D0847671

Painting and Our Inner World

The Psychology of Image Making

The Plenum Series in Adult Development and Aging

SERIES EDITOR:
Jack Demick, *University of Massachusetts Medical School, Worcester, Massachusetts*

ADULT DEVELOPMENT, THERAPY, AND CULTURE
A Postmodern Synthesis
Gerald D. Young

THE CHANGING NATURE OF PAIN COMPLAINTS OVER THE LIFESPAN
Michael R. Thomas and Ranjan Roy

THE DEVELOPMENT OF LOGIC IN ADULTHOOD
Postformal Thought and Its Applications
Jan D. Sinnott

HANDBOOK OF ADULT DEVELOPMENT
Edited by Jack Demick and Carrie Andreoletti

HANDBOOK OF AGING AND MENTAL HEALTH
An Integrative Approach
Edited by Jacob Lomranz

HANDBOOK OF CLINICAL GEROPSYCHOLOGY
Edited by Michel Hersen and Vincent B. Van Hasselt

HUMAN DEVELOPMENT AND THE SPIRITUAL LIFE
How Consciousness Grows Toward Transformation
Ronald R. Irwin

HUMAN DEVELOPMENT IN ADULTHOOD
Lewis R. Aiken

PAINTING AND OUR INNER WORLD
The Psychology of Image Making
Pavel Machotka

A Continuation Order Plan is available for this series. A continuation order will bring delivery of each new volume immediately upon publication. Volumes are billed only upon actual shipment. For further information please contact the publisher.

Painting and Our Inner World

The Psychology of Image Making

Pavel Machotka

University of California, Santa Cruz
Santa Cruz, California

with the collaboration of

Lori Felton

Kluwer Academic/Plenum Publishers
New York • Boston • Dordrecht • London • Moscow

Library of Congress Cataloging-in-Publication Data

Machotka, Pavel.
    Painting and our inner world: the psychology of image making/Pavel Machotka.
        p.   cm. — (The Plenum series in adult development and aging)
    Includes bibliographical references and index.
    ISBN 0-306-47408-5
        1. Art—Psychology.   2. Personality and creative ability.   3. Meaning (Psychology)   I.
    Title.   II. Series.

    N71 .M233 2003
    701'.15—dc21

                                                                                        2002042767

ISBN: 0-306-47408-5

©2003 Kluwer Academic / Plenum Publishers, New York
233 Spring Street, New York, New York 10013

http://www.wkap.nl

10   9   8   7   6   5   4   3   2   1

A C.I.P. record for this book is available from the Library of Congress

Permissions for books published in Europe: *permissions@wkap.nl*
Permissions for books published in the United States of America:
permissions@wkap.com

Printed in the United States of America

Acknowledgments

From its inception, this research has borne the imprint of the many contributions of Lori Felton. She helped formulate the questions that we would attempt to answer and the methods by which we would address them, and worked with several of the participants to gather the information we needed. At the beginning, Lori was joined by Cynthia DuVal, and we three set the direction of the study; to both of them I am grateful for the fruitful beginnings. Cynthia left town after two years with the project, but Lori stayed with it for six years, gathering further data and above all helping interpret it. Interpretation is a matter of two qualities that need to be opposed and balanced—clinical sensitivity and critical reflection—and Lori's balance was exemplary; for the final statistical analysis, she helped perfect the rating form for the images and then assess them; and she helped define the characteristics of several of the clusters. For all of these contributions I am deeply grateful.

This book is also the product of intensive work with individual participants, work that had to be entrusted to selected senior students in psychology who wished to spend a year gaining research experience. While it was my responsibility to train them carefully, it became theirs to work reliably and quite independently. The trust I placed in them was repaid with thorough information on each participant; without it, neither the individual interpretations we had reached nor the overall analysis I report here would have been possible, and to them I wish to express my warm thanks as well. Over the years of the project, they were the following:

Analisa Adelberg

Michelle Bryant

Heinrich Dierschke

Lara Goldenberg

Carli Hartmann

Molly Hibbert

Lisa Knoop

Paulette Lucier

Florence Landau

Shauna Lawrence

Ellyn Lee

Vanessa Quinn

Andrew Penn

Peter Plessas

Julie Poyton

Faris Sabbah

Anna Schlote

Gudrun Stangl

Mariam Toor

Henry Yang

In the later years of the project, Harley Baker joined us, at first as an informal participant and later as an indispensable consultant: it was his expertise that ensured that the cluster analysis was done correctly. Both for the conception and for the high standards in its execution, my cordial thanks.

Contents

Introduction

Art, the Body, and Relationships

Yet, at my age—about seventy—the color sensations that pro-
duce light are the cause of the abstractions which prevent me
from covering my canvas fully, or pursuing the delimitation of
objects where their points of contact are tenuous and delicate.
—PAUL CÉZANNE, LETTER TO EMILE BERNARD, OCTOBER 23, 1905
(DORAN, 1978)

Of the complex of motives, predispositions, hesitations, and talents that
Cézanne may have brought to his pursuit of painting, we are allowed to
glimpse at least one clearly: the matter of contact between independent
color patches. In the last decade of his life he developed a manner of
painting in which he set down separate patches of color in various parts
of his canvas, suggesting the forms of the landscape he was studying
and yet creating a rhythmical surface which was formally satisfying. It
was a mode of drawing, painting, and creating a dynamic composition
at the same time; but it required that the patches be brought together.

Here was the rub: the patches, as they came into contact, presented
the difficulty to which the quote refers. He is describing it to the young
painter Bernard, who had visited him, talked with him at length about
painting, and then asked him more questions by correspondence.
When they were together, Cézanne had revealed something else about
the problem of contact, albeit inadvertently: it was his acute fear of
being touched. When Bernard once restrained him from falling,
Cézanne ran off frightened and angry, and nearly broke off relations. He
soon apologized, of course, but his housekeeper had to explain to
Bernard that it was nothing personal, that Cézanne simply could not
bear to have people touch him.

Cézanne's late stylistic question—this question at least—was therefore a mirror of a psychological question. It is as if, by some unavoidable connection, the aesthetic problems faced while painting were also a metaphor for dilemmas in the life of the painter. May we not take this as a more general suggestion? To understand the stylistic questions painters bring to paintings, should we not look at their patterns of intimate relationships—relationships remembered, wished for, or experienced now? Might not the inner representation of relationships become a kind of map for at least some aspects of visual form?

Not only Cézanne's words but certain theoretical writings, too, prepare us for this idea. The aesthetic writings of Adrian Stokes (1966), a psychoanalytic critic, find images of the human body even in the most abstract artistic representations. We respond bodily to the rough and smooth texture of architecture and to the benign form of the inhabitable tower and the malign form of the bloated gasometer. To read Stokes's work is to be persuaded by the inevitability of projecting the qualities of the body—goodness and badness, masculinity and femininity, convexness and concavity, among others—into the visual world.

By a related theoretical argument, Stokes also explores the importance of relationships for the way in which we experience the world at large, and art perhaps most insistently. He distinguishes between two modes of relating to the world, the part-object mode and the whole-object mode; in the first, objects exist only by virtue of their connection to our wishes, while in the second they are accepted as independent. The first implies a kind of wishful merging, as seen in the close involvement with a painting's subject or the wish to walk around in its space; this wish seems to begin with the infant's initial confusion between his and his mother's body. A respect for the work's independence, on the other hand—seeing it as a whole, being able to look at it critically and without its relation to our needs—is akin to the infant's maturing acceptance of the mother's separateness.

Whether or not the adult aesthetic response is rooted that deeply in childhood seems to me secondary: what does matter is that Stokes's psychological aesthetics is suggestive of that experience, and yes, persuasive by its insistence on our bodily relation to art, and by its evocation of our experience of relationships even as we respond to art.

We are prepared, then, to find images of relationships—of the body to the world and of the self to others—in the abstract properties of our visual productions. We need not look for anything quite so universal as Stokes's dimension of merging vs. separateness, because by itself it fails to account for differences between people, nor as specific as Cézanne's problem with contact, because relationships can be problematic not only at the body boundary but further away as well. But we can look—and in this research we did look—for ways in which a person's patterning of relationships is connected to image making.

Ultimately my wish is to understand painting, but in this study we explored a practical analog of it: the transformation of photographed scenes into artistic images on the computer. The word "painting" is, however, both brief and evocative, so it serves well, and in any case the making of images that I report here does share a lot with literal painting: the ability to use color, the invitation to use one's hand expressively, the possible emphasis on surface, texture and composition, and above all the need to address the issue of representation vs. abstraction. I hope that what our participants brought to the images they made for us will apply to the narrower act of painting as well.

The task I chose to mirror painting had to be accessible to a broad variety of people. The participants were therefore essentially unselected except for their interest in the study and a desire to participate in it, and this meant that, by design, they would be variously accomplished in art and unequally creative. This, from a psychological point of view, seemed most important: it seemed right that *all* struggles to achieve form have an equal claim on our interest, and that a broad spectrum of such attempts would teach us more than a narrow one. Had the study been limited to highly creative or quite accomplished individuals, for example, it might have placed an artificial limit on what we would learn.

The image makers, beside being connected by their desire to participate, were also close in age, having been recruited for the most part from undergraduate classes. But they varied in the senses that counted most, namely that some were deeply committed to art while others had done none before, and their personalities spanned the broad range one would expect from large undergraduate populations.

My collaborators and I came to feel justified in this choice because the images the participants produced came to vary considerably, as did the personalities they brought to the process. We also came to value the length of time we spent with each person: not only was the information we gathered rich, and quite susceptible to cogent interpretation, but each individual remained interested in the study over the weeks or months before we had finished. We think that, whatever their previous experience with art, the tasks we set for them challenged them adequately and with rare exceptions brought out their best efforts. This meant that the engagement of their personality seemed all the more genuine.

We studied each person as if he or she were going to be our only one. We chose a task that was intuitively understandable and free from the anxiety that sometimes accompanies image making: after training them in using complex retouching software on the computer, we gave them a choice of photographs of landscapes and asked them to transform the chosen one into "a work of art". This process, equally poised between the constructive and the destructive, seemed both playful and responsible, and they generally fell to it. We took copious notes on the process, asked the image makers to comment on what they were doing, and at the end asked further questions about what they had just done and experienced.

Later we asked them to return for an interview, which was psychodynamically oriented and focused both on the handling of drives and affects (such as love, aggression, and assertiveness) and on the memories, images, ideals, and experiences of relationships; this is described at greater length in Chapter 2 and Appendix B. We recorded and transcribed the interview for future analysis.

To interpret a person's work, we first reviewed the record of image making, noted what seemed salient about the process and the product, and jotted down questions we hoped might be answered by the interview. When the interview transcript was available, we studied its salient themes and attempted to find any connections there might be with the earlier notes on the image making. This was always done in a group, with all the assistants from a given year working together.

When we had tested 72 people, over a period of five years, we had also arrived at that many individual interpretations. In each interpretation some prominent need (for example, compensation or trauma mastery) or some stylistic consistency (perhaps an emphasis on boundaries) or some integrative wish (to join everything through consistent form) appeared as salient. *These disparate connections were suddenly unified, however, if we looked at them as representations of remembered or wished for relationships.* They could be viewed as images of a wish-fulfilling, or avoidant, or yet of a reparative or complying relationship. Admittedly, to see matters this way we needed to entertain a broad view of the meaning of the term "relationship": it had to refer not only to intimate relationships but also to body boundaries between oneself and others and relations to the world at large.

However satisfactory it was to have found this kind of meaning in the individual images, this was not our only aim. It was no less important to see if there was a pattern by which the *types* of image making might be related to *kinds* of meanings. If there was a pattern, it would confirm the connections we had seen individually, and incidentally it would be easier to discuss and remember. This is normally a research dilemma: one either attends to the complexities of individual psychodynamics, or one looks for a system by which personality types correlate with artistic production. The first approach limits the number of people one can study, while the second precludes an understanding of any single individual. Here, we have attempted to combine both and reap the benefits of each.

To see if there were patterns of meaning connected to types of images, we had to start with the images themselves; we had to ask whether what we could observe in them and glean from the record of their making would cluster into coherent groups. We coded the appearance of each image and the record of its construction, and with this on hand performed a cluster analysis, which, briefly put for now, did group the images into seven clusters; they were consistent internally and distinct from each other externally. Then came the crucial part: to see if the seven groupings of images reflected that many ways of relating to the world. If they did—if the individual interpretations were consistent within the clusters and different between them—then we would be all the more confident of the interpretations, and that much clearer about the metaphorical transformation of relationships into the forms of art.

Happily, that is what we did find. Each of the seven image types could now be called a psychological style of image making, and in this report could form a natural chapter; together they constitute the core of our findings. Within each chapter, I build up a picture of the cluster through a quick look at the individuals who make it up, and then turn to two detailed case histories which represent its characteristics best. In this way I remain close to the complexities of individual psychodynamics—which was the starting point and remains the ultimate reference point. The seven chapters are preceded by a conceptual and methodological introduction (Chapters 1 and 2), and succeeded by a conclusion (Chapter 10) and appendices; in the concluding chapter I step away from the clusters, take a more integrative view of the psychology of image making, and connect the styles seen in this analysis with styles observed in the world of art.

CHAPTER 1

Artists and Their Biographies

Well before the interest in the possible psychological purposes of art, and quite likely as a precursor of it, there developed an interest in the personality of the artist. We take it as axiomatic that the latter came with the Renaissance, and this for two quite simple reasons: artists not only ceased being anonymous, they also came to be understood and valued as individuals with ambitions and peculiarities—and style. When Vasari was persuaded in 1546 by Cardinal Alexander Farnese to write a history of modern art, he set out to discuss individually all the Florentine artists whom he considered important (and some from outside Florence, as long as they could claim a connection) and to list their most important works. But the "lives" in the three-volume book that resulted are more like résumés than biographies, and they are made individual only by their brief introductions, each of which attempts to capture some essential quality of the artist or his fate. Thus Simone Martini is introduced with these words:

> Most truly may those men be called happy who are by nature disposed to the cultivation of the arts, for not only may they derive great honour and profit therefrom in their lives, but what is more important, they secure never-dying fame. Still more fortunate are they who to such dispositions add a character and manners calculated to render them acceptable to all men ... . (Lanvin, *Vasari*, 1550/1967)

From this we learn something of Simone's dedication, felicitous manners, and ultimate fame, but little that might explain their connection with his manner of painting. Vasari is in fact more interested in how each painter contributed to the development of lifelike representation—that triumph of high Renaissance art—than in the painter's style. Only indirectly do we learn anything that might

7

connect character with style, as when he describes Andrea del Castagno (unjustly, as has come to light) as envious, cruel, and fiend-like, and in another passage calls his coloring crude and harsh; we are left to suppose a connection if we wish. We are similarly free to marvel at the variety of personalities that did become artists, but if we do so, that will be our conclusion, not Vasari's purpose. We can read some psychology into this fact, but it is difficult to imagine that a contemporary reader would have done so.

If, at the time, the obvious diversity of characters who painted did not lead to an implied psychology of painting, a full two and a half centuries later the nascent notion of art as the expression of feeling did. The notion was the product of the Romantic movement and we can trace one of its first expressions to Wordsworth, who in the year 1800 defined poetry as "the spontaneous overflow of powerful feelings" (Spitz, 1985a). By introducing the artist's motives into the creation of poetry, Wordsworth called attention to the artist's person— rather than, for example, to his attainment of a certain level of excellence, as Vasari had done—and indirectly justified the individuality of style. But we should note that Wordsworth's conception of the spontaneous overflow emphasized that which was common to all artists' motives—particularly Romantic artists—not what was individual, and that it was not until the formulation of psychodynamic theory that a foundation was laid for studying the connection between the artists' personalities and their art. By this I refer to a psychological connection between the personal dynamics (motives and ways of dealing with them) and the artist's work, based in a coherent theory, rather than to the kind of individual connections implied in many excellent biographies. Many of the latter may well offer observations that fit their subject better than a general theory would, but there are simply too many to survey—any general library database is likely to reveal over 10,000 books with the words "life and work" in their title.

THE VICISSITUDES OF PSYCHODYNAMICS

Freud's views on art, whether accepted, revised, or rejected, were, in fact, rooted in the Romantic era (Spitz, 1985a). Certainly the notion of art as an expression of feelings or wishes which are inadequately expressed in real life, which is clearly implied in the notion of displacement as seen in dreams and symptoms, is not very different from the notion of "overflow".[1] To be sure, the psychodynamic notion is potentially much richer inasmuch as it is presented in the context of conflict theory and the individual structure of ego-defenses, but in its simplest form it relies on unsatisfied motives.

In its subtler forms, however, it says more. In his essay "Creative writers and daydreaming," Freud (1908) first stated a version of the "expressive" theory when he compared the creation of the work of art to child's play and daydreaming, each of which fulfills wishes not permitted in reality or granted by it. But he also drew a distinction between fantasy and art which lent his view a complexity whose importance is often underestimated. He said that the artist, unlike the daydreamer, clothed his fantasy in the aesthetic devices of which he was a master, which made the fantasy both acceptable and attractive to the reader. Of course the satisfactions from wishes represented in fantasy were, for Freud, always primary, and those from aesthetic devices secondary, but in recognizing the latter at all he made clear that wishes were not everything and that the ego had much important work to do in creating art and reacting to it. In fact he left open—for others—the possibility that the ego's work is the more individual and interesting. This has encouraged students of personality to attempt to understand the creation of works of art by looking for reflections of the artist's ego—of his or her manner of handling impulses.

This is, of course, one of the principal concerns of this research; the ego's work will be given equal importance to the motives which impel it. But as I had said in the Introduction, the concern will be even broader: to look into representations that bring the ego's work together, that is, representations that reflect the pattern of interpersonal relationships—remembered, experienced in the present, wished for—that serves as

---

[1] To illustrate how close Freud's views were to Wordsworth's, Spitz quotes the following two passages (1985a):

> What is a poet? ... He is a man speaking to men: a man, it is true, endowed with more lively sensibility, more enthusiasm and tenderness, who has a greater knowledge of human nature, and a more comprehensive soul than are supposed to be common among mankind ... . (Wordsworth, Preface to *Lyrical Ballads* of 1800, 1950, p. 684)

> ... creative writers are valuable allies and their evidence is to be prized highly, for they are apt to know a whole host of things between heaven and earth of which our philosophy has not yet let us dream. In their knowledge of the mind they are far in advance of us everyday people, for they draw upon sources which we have not yet opened up for science. (Freud, *Delusions and Dreams in Jensen's "Gradiva,"* 1907, p. 8)

a kind of map for the person's metaphorical translations into aesthetic form. I shall be more specific when I describe our methods in the next chapter.

Returning to psychodynamic theory, however, I must also say that Freud was careful to point out the limitations of psychoanalytic inquiry. In none of his comments on art or artists did he claim to explain more than a part of the artist's work. Artists, like ordinary persons, may be neurotic and weighed down by the rigidities of their past, and that is a proper subject for psychoanalysis; it may even illuminate some aspects of their work, particularly that which is repetitive or rigid. But, unlike ordinary people, artists have a gift for transforming their inner world in an active and fruitful way, and this way is in itself unanalyzable. This is the "problem of the creative artist [before which] analysis must, alas, lay down its arms" (Freud, 1928).

So even Freud had theoretical reasons for leaving part of the artist's work unexplained. Those reasons apply to the present report as well. Part of the image makers' work will be explained—by its relation to personality—but another part will remain unexplainable or unpredictable; it may be attributable to talent, invention, favorable circumstances, or something else, and those matters are either given, or novel, or fortuitous. It is not a question of not knowing enough about the person, but a question of being unable to account for the *new* in creative work in terms that are designed to account for the old. (This is a problem for all science, not psychology in general or psychoanalysis in particular.) Freud was even careful to express doubts about the possibility of reconstructing the artist's intentions reliably, when in the essay *The Moses of Michelangelo* he made this reflection:

> What if we have taken too serious and profound a view of the details which were nothing to the artist, details which he had introduced quite arbitrarily or for some purely formal reasons with no hidden intention behind? What if we have shared the fate of so many interpreters who have thought they saw quite clearly things which the artist did not intend either consciously or unconsciously? I cannot tell.

The uncertainty of interpretation is a caution worth observing, and I shall observe it; nevertheless, I shall also be able to rely on things about our art-making individuals that we can observe clearly. Where we see parallels between, for example, an artist's view of interpersonal relationships and an emphasis on the interconnections of the elements in a painting, we will feel justified in assuming a connection between them; and when we find the problem of intimacy handled differently by artists making one kind of image than another, we will not hesitate to presume a functional connection. A healthy respect for artistic creation and the right amount of modesty about the completeness of interpretation are no less necessary than a dogged search for credible evidence.

Psychodynamic theory has therefore left ample space for formulations broader than its original ones: for motives such as reparation, for the pleasure of exercising one's sensory faculties, for the security of constructing an interface between one's wishes and harsh reality, and for the sheer delight in play. One has but to consult a thorough review, such as the two written by Spitz (1985a,b), to follow the best of the developments. And it has left room for a change in emphasis from drives and their vicissitudes to interpersonal relations and their emotional consequences. As far as the present work is concerned, relations with others may provide the best explanation for the metaphorical meanings of forms in the visual arts. I say this not out of theoretical preference or partisanship, but for the simple reason that the representation of relationships is more likely to constitute a map than would the image of one's needs; this map—probably as visceral and kinesthetic as it is cognitive—can in turn more easily serve as a source of visual metaphors.

RESEARCH ON INDIVIDUALS AND THE QUESTION OF TYPES

The motives for creating, and the styles in which one creates, can seem theoretically nearly infinite. This is not in itself unfortunate, because it may reflect reality, but it is certainly confusing. If one does what psychodynamic investigations do best, which is to focus closely on individuals, one may come to wish that a bit of forest might become discernible behind the trees; to put the matter in another way, even if the cornerstone of theory and the ultimate object of understanding remains the individual, some simpler account of a more general process would be desirable. The cluster analysis—the types of image making—reported here will reflect that need. To introduce the issue of types, and to present some of the previous psychodynamic work that bears on this study, we can look at the manner in which individual variation has been simplified in the past.

TYPES IN THE STUDY OF ART MAKING

One mode of transcending the idiosyncratic view is to contrast at least two individuals. A contrast will be more persuasive than a single account when differences in the explanatory variables, such as aspects of personality, lead to differences in effects, such as painterly style. If two artists differ in, let us say, rigidity of defense, and the more rigid artist has a single, unchanging style while the less rigid one changes his style easily, then we have that much more reason to believe that defenses help explain their styles. I have done just such a study with two contemporary painters—my friends and painting colleagues—and connected their painterly style to the cognitive style revealed by the Rorschach. To make sure that only style, rather than subject matter, was at issue, I took advantage of a natural experiment in which the two painters painted habitually side-by-side *en plein air*. I watched them at work, described their approach to the painting from the first setup to the finished canvas, and independently had the Rorschach administered by someone who knew neither the painters nor their work (Machotka, 1999).

The Rorschach examiner, Stephanie Dudek, familiar with the cognitive profiles of artists through her own research, went beyond her normal assessment and ventured some guesses about the artists' styles of painting. It is as much a tribute to her intimate knowledge of the test as to the power of cognitive style to influence the way one paints that her predictions were uncannily accurate. Thus a cognitive style we might call repressive because of its deliberate answers, long reaction time, and firmness of percept once it was formed, went with a painterly style recognized by its definitive brush strokes, clear edges, well defined compositional emphases, clearly anticipated color effects, and no changes in the painting once it was under way—in short, a style of a single, clear intention maintained throughout the process of painting. A quite different Rorschach style—obviously impulsive because it was rambling and imprecise, and full of eruptions of primary process— characterized the painter who did little initial planning, plunged in, remained quick and imprecise, and frequently changed direction.

Such observations make the connection between the artist's work and an aspect of his personality more credible than would a single narrative. To make the connection, one uses not only the logic of comparison but also the logic of limited variables—say, one aspect of the person and one aspect of the work; what one gives up is the richness of the whole life and the entire *oeuvre*. But if the variables are important enough intrinsically, and connected closely enough with psychodynamic theory, then some aspect of the theory is illuminated and some of the artistic work explained. In this tradition I would also locate Dudek's own studies of Rorschach styles and styles in painting and architecture (Dudek and Hall, 1979; Dudek and Marchand, 1983).

Abstracting from the individual Rorschach protocols of the painters, she and Marchand established a continuum of weak to strong cognitive controls, and found that the weaker controls accompanied more impulsive styles, while stronger controls indicated more constricted styles. Such findings, while more abstract than my study of the two painters, are nevertheless consistent, and likewise use the logic of comparison.

In their study of architects, however, Dudek and Hall made finer distinctions and discerned several Rorschach styles. As an example, a "gestural" Rorschach style, which indicated powerful drives and unstable controls, characterized an architectural style that was bold, exuberant, sensual and dynamic. A "vital, imaginative, and controlled" style—expressive and balanced, different from the first but not at opposite ends from it—was reflected in a neo-classical architectural manner. The logic of such a study is most useful, because it does not depend on mere opposition—which, while clarifying, also simplifies unduly—but rather posits several modes of creating and is more plausible on its face. The same logic dictated our own analysis of the artistic work and personality of our painters.

TYPES IN THE STUDY OF
ARTISTIC BIOGRAPHY

While these findings encourage us to look for a complex typology, rather than a bipolar one, it is not clear just how complex it should ideally be. I have tried to look at the matter theoretically, starting with the dramatic differences that leap to the eyes between painters, and the styles that follow, and come up with a minimum of four types (1992). This would have been merely a thoughtful exercise if it did not also connect, now, with three of the patterns that appear in this study. This argues that the search for types is useful, provided that they are fine enough and account for enough of the evidence without too much distortion. Surely the number four is too small, but because of the close connection between three of them and the clusters that appear here, they are worth outlining (and returning to, in the final chapter, with more evidence at hand).

In the theoretical paper I had presumed that there would be a pattern in which a sufficient *rigidity of defense* would bring a painter's life and work very close to each other because both are similarly constricted. No painter illustrates this better than Piet Mondrian, whose whole life, as well as his artistic career, seemed to move toward a kind of antiseptic abstraction. A lifelong bachelor of meticulously correct

and neat habits, he often fell in love but was never intimate; an enthu-
siastic dancer, he danced only the new dances, thanks to their formality, balance, and tightness, and only at arms' length. His life and his art
seemed one: cultivated life, as he saw it, was turning away from the
natural toward the abstract (Gay, 1976). This pattern, it turns out, is
represented in this work by cluster 7 (see Chapter 9), in which the need
for abstract representation reflects the same avoidance of emotion and
physical contact.

In a second pattern a painful, *early loss* might serve not as a
stylistic guide but as a motivating force for a focused dedication to
a certain kind of painting. This pattern, too, has its clear exemplar,
René Magritte, who at age thirteen saw his mother drowned; she was
naked except for her face, which was covered by her nightgown. He
later organized his life around an unvarying routine and was literally
never parted from his wife's side. In his paintings, women are often
partly dead, partly alive, or partly animate and partly inanimate, or yet
half fish, half human. The uncanny surrealism is in many ways highly
original, but in other ways it is a close reflection of his psychic reality
and, we would say, his attempts to master it (Spitz, 1985a). Neither
so dramatic a loss nor so great a dedication to personal safety and
a narrowly focused aesthetic program need be anticipated among our
participants, but the work of two clusters (the first and second,
described in Chapters 3 and 4) does represent attempts to handle loss—
but, as we shall see, in two quite distinct ways.

In another pattern it is not motives but *permeable boundaries* that
play the crucial role: an unclear sense of self, defining oneself through
one's relation to others, and alternating between clinging and pushing
away and between idealization and disillusionment. They characterize
the so-called borderline personality, and are illustrated by Picasso.
Inseparable as a boy from his father and as a man from other artists, he
found it hard to do his art when alone; even the invention of Cubism
was the result of a very close collaboration with Braque. His sadistic
feelings of a given moment might betray themselves in a painting of a
woman, and his anger might appear in pictures of bulls destroying
everything about them. As a result, his painting is a kind of autobiography: a carefully dated record of his feelings (Gedo, 1980). This
pattern did not appear here, and it is possible that it is fairly rare; it
may well depend on a rare combination of a borderline organization
and extreme talent.

The fourth pattern, unlike the first three, works freely, whether
in response to impulses, philosophical convictions, ethical concerns,
or even a patron's commission—and it works, variably and quite

unpredictably, from imagination rather than constraint. It is the *dynamic of robust health*, and Rubens is the artist one can reasonably cite in evidence. He felt deeply, read widely, behaved ethically, exercised, and had two very productive careers—the lesser known one being that of a diplomat. His emotionally gratifying life was, in other words, joined to a full mobilization of creative energy. The consequence for his art was that we cannot understand it in terms of sublimation; there seemed nothing to sublimate. His female nudes are joyful, abundant, generous, yes, but also frank and unselfconscious, neither inviting nor coy; rather they portray a variety of emotional or even ethical states (White, 1980; Clark, 1984). Perhaps this type is as unusual as Rubens was himself, and need not be anticipated in so clear a form here, but there will be a few striking resemblances between the boldness of the style of cluster 4 (Chapter 6) and the availability of emotion that animates its painters.

TYPES IN THIS STUDY

But such patterns, although highly visible, cannot describe all that we found and cannot serve as a basis for ordering it. Nor would any other theoretical ordering, it seemed, because it would obscure too much of what should remain visible. It became clear that here the patterns should be allowed to emerge more naturally from the range of individual results themselves. We grouped the images, as I said, by a cluster analysis, which gave us seven image types (a number, it must be added, that would have been smaller if we had had fewer participants and larger if we had had more). What is important is that the image types and the individual psychodynamics should correspond, which, I may say in advance, they do very satisfactorily (and reliably, in that they survive the test of independent analysis; see Appendix A). And it is equally important that they be connected to the world of art: to artists such as Max Beckmann, Alberto Giacometti, Paul Cézanne, Henri Rousseau, and the artist-psychologist Marion Milner, all of whom join Rubens and Mondrian to broaden our creative horizon.

To this discussion of types should be added a psychodynamic comment which will at first appear as a peculiar complication. In an earlier work, based on a similar study of personality but designed to explain aesthetic preferences, I discovered that almost *all* attachment to aesthetic objects was accompanied by some limitation on one's capacity for intimacy (Machotka, 1979). Admittedly, this was more of a vivid observation than a careful test, but it has been verified, by other methods, by Babbage and Valentine (1995). While this makes sense from the general psychodynamic view of art as displacement, it also has the effect of blurring the differences between people rather than sharpening them.

The apparent complication turns into an advantage, however, and in fact helps us appreciate this book's most subtle findings. If from one point of view inhibition of intimacy is quite common and helps turn people toward art for their emotional satisfactions, from a subtler point of view the inhibitions are likely to be different in kind; they may reveal different images of relationships, varying hopes and idealizations, and even excessive needs to merge intimately with others. The matter of relationships, in other words, is much too complex to be understood adequately by the concept of inhibition, and all of these variations turn out to be reflected, each in its own way, in the different image styles. The findings are quite clear on this: in each of the clusters of images, there are characteristic patterns of relating that help explain the forms the images take. *I propose, more clearly than could have been anticipated, that the image of interpersonal relationships is a kind of map by which aesthetic reality can be ordered and understood, and indeed that the relationships one seeks to create between the elements of a visual image ultimately stand for one's interpersonal world.*

CHAPTER 2

Image Makers and Their Purposes

Our Methods

If our interest is in the psychodynamic contributions to the manner and substance of image making, then our first task is to find a way of making images that is interesting and accessible equally to people trained and untrained in art, and our second is to assess personality in a manner consistent with what we are looking for.

IMAGE MAKING ON THE COMPUTER

To produce images, blank paper and some crayons would not have been out of the question, but they would have had the disadvantage of favoring those who have had experience with drawing and painting. Anyone inexperienced with filling a sheet or canvas with images will recall the inhibition, perhaps even the terror, of facing the blankness and being expected to fill it. The alternative became clear several years ago when it turned out that what used to be quite esoteric ways of manipulating photographs had become highly perfected and perfectly accessible. With the Adobe Photoshop program one can take an image and perform a multitude of transformations of it: moving objects from place to place, adding objects from other pictures, changing an element's size or color or orientation, and changing the texture of any portion of the photograph to something more schematic, random, or stylized. This very brief list of possibilities hardly does the program justice, but it suggests the central idea: people making images should have the opportunity of working with an existing photograph so as to change it freely into something they could call art. We thought that if they feared a blank canvas because of what had to be added to it, they might feel at ease with a photograph they could alter, add to, or even ruin. This proved to be right; the task was seen as meaningful and the participants settled into it without difficulty.

We—Lori Felton, Cynthia DuVal and I—learned the rudiments of the program, taught it to a few pilot subjects, and over several months settled upon a procedure we would use for what turned out to be one year of pilot work and five years of actual testing. As far as the image-making part was concerned, we settled on the following:

(a) We selected six photographs of landscapes to represent different visual challenges—different initial levels of organization, varying color schemes, and varied distances from the observer. Of these, one would be used for training (see Fig. 1) and the other five for actual testing (see Figs 2–6); and because the Photoshop software came with a flower still life to demonstrate the program, we added it to the collection (Fig. 7).

(b) The participants were first given a tutorial in which they could try the basic manual operations, which included drawing with the "pencil", painting with the "brush", "erasing", and duplicating various parts of the image; they then practiced some of the many transformations provided by the software program under the category of "filters".

Figure 1. Temple—Training Picture
Note.   **Color images of Figures 1 through 74 in this volume can be found on the author's website: http://www.machotka.com.**

Figure 2. Village

Figure 3. Sicily

Figure 4. Hillside

Figure 5. Leaves

Figure 6. Garden

Figure 7. Still life

These—in ever increasing numbers with succeeding versions of the program—would alter the textures, outline the edges, add random pixels, and variously shape the areas being worked on. This was the minimum that all image makers were taught, but since they were free to explore whatever other operations they wished, their training became individual in response to their varying curiosity; and starting with the minimal hour or so, their training also varied in length, with some people faster and others slower, and some curious and others less so. All were, however, very much interested in the program and eager to go on to the next phases. This—the interest they felt as well as the variability they themselves introduced—is how we wished it to be.

(c) They then returned for the actual testing, with the same experimenter, whose overall aim was as simple as it was undefined: they knew they would be asked to "make a work of art" from one of the photographs in Figs 2–7. We explained of course that the meaning of the term was personal and that it was typical for them to discover the meaning only while working, and we never found a person to be puzzled or inhibited by our request; everyone found something to do. A few insisted on working with the training picture, and we simply accepted the choice. I should say, however, that while everyone got right into the task, their approach for the most part had little to do with the visual "challenges" I thought I had seen in the photographs and much to do with whatever fantasies they allowed themselves to entertain. (Some of the art students did respond to the visual challenge, but also imposed their own concerns upon it.) We discovered, for example, that the photograph of the Village (Fig. 2) evoked images of the family, so dominant were the big buildings on the hill and so childlike, and sibling-like, the buildings in the valley. That picture, more than the others, was like a Thematic Apperception picture (Murray, 1963), and the content of the responses to it could be explained by memories or images of the family. But there were also stylistic responses to it which were made possible by the opportunity to transform it.

(d) While the participant worked, the experimenter took careful notes on each operation, indicating the Photoshop tool used, the operation performed, the result, and any comments made. The participants were told that we were interested in their comments on what they were doing, and if they did not volunteer them, they would be asked; this procedure had varied success because some people were highly verbal and others almost not at all. The experimenters in any case never asked for explanations, only for comments on "what was going on." The time elapsed was also noted, and images in progress were saved in such a way that we could reconstruct the picture's development when we needed to. When they were done—as they saw it—they answered a series of questions about the process itself, their intentions, the image's possible meaning, and their past experience with the making or viewing of art (see Appendix B, "Post-image interview").

As soon as the protocol recording the process was available, the experimenter would present a detailed summary of the picture-making, stage by stage, and the whole group of experimenters working together in any particular year would attempt to reconstruct the painter's intentions, comment on the style and composition, ask provisional questions about the image's contents, and react to the image's aesthetic quality. While the reactions of the members of the group were quite individual, they also converged on a few themes, and in any case were all noted for future reference, that is, for future linkages with the image maker's personality once that was revealed. This work by the group was a productive and mutually stimulating exchange of ideas and an excellent learning experience for the undergraduate experimenters.

PERSONALITY

Although "personality" is a broader term than necessary, it is a useful shorthand for locating this research in a certain tradition. As much as one has to admire the current attempts to establish personality dimensions that have a certain claim to universality (McCrae and Costa, 1997), for understanding the dynamics underlying image making I find more useful a view of personality which emphasizes process, conflict, memories of relations to others and wishes connected with them. I also value using methods which—and this needs to be emphasized—allow room for surprises. The most significant issues that animate a person may, in my view, be revealed in unpredictable ways, as in response to the question, "what are your prominent fears?"— a question which may have meaning only for a certain number of persons. Any measure designed to leave room for such findings must cast its net fairly wide and allow open-ended, detailed, answers.

Our main diagnostic instrument was therefore a psychodynamic interview. It assumes that one's handling of needs and emotions, particularly as they relate to people significant in one's life, is of central significance. I had used it in earlier research (Machotka, 1979), where it served to assess the dominant emotional and interpersonal issues of the participants, and could successfully be connected with a person's aesthetic choices. It was adapted for use here. Although relatively brief—about an hour and a half to two hours in length—it nevertheless was indicative enough of what animated the individuals emotionally: the memory of their relation to their parents, the images and the reality of their romantic and other relationships in the present, the patterns by which they had been disciplined, the parents' goals for them, their own ideas, goals, and hopes for the future, and similar issues (see Appendix B, "Outline of psychodynamic interview").

To minimize experimenter bias—in this case, a projection of the experimenter's personality both on the picture produced and psychodynamic material elicited—we made sure that a different experimenter did the interview than was present at the image making. All were trained by us in practice interviews to ask questions matter-of-factly and to probe for details, and all took turns doing all the procedures. The interview was then transcribed and distributed to the whole group, to be read in advance of the next meeting and discussed there.

INDIVIDUAL INTERPRETATION

Referring to what we had deemed worthy of attention in the image, we would now pull out of the interview any material that seemed thematically or functionally related. It was a kind of clinical interpretation, one in which we looked for patterns, resonances, or echoes, in the manner of a clinician (and for that matter any sensitive biographer) attempting to make sense of an individual's life. It was ultimately a process of searching for each person's pattern of relations to others, interests, concerns, presuppositions, fears, and ultimate wishes, insofar as they related to the image we had studied. In other words, while the process was intuitive, it was also focused—on linkages between the personality and the image that had been produced—and this guaranteed a certain discipline in the theorizing.

Working in groups—if the discussion is kept from moving too quickly toward closure, which was my task—has the advantage that no major connection will go unnoticed; groups tend to notice first one connection, then another, contest some, and recast others. Even so, the outcome was not always theoretically neat: with some participants, a playful or obsessive style might seem the most important matter to note, while with others it might be a stubborn memory of traumatic events. It was only when the final cluster analysis was done that we could also extract from the individual interpretations what they had in common, namely the kind of map of relations to the world that we were looking for.

I must convey here a sense of profound satisfaction with this process: *we always felt that we had come to understand a significant part of the individual's productions through some aspect of his or her psychological functioning.* That this process was not illusory was, of course, only shown later: in part by the reliability study, in part by the success of the cluster analysis. There were, of course, many areas of the participants' functioning that could not be revealed to us in the brief time we had together[1] or would slip through our net through mistakes, but enough was available, as objective fact or psychological datum, for us to feel felt we had a convincing psychodynamic interpretation, however limited, on each person.

EXPERIMENTERS AND IMAGE MAKERS

Given the requirements of the undergraduate psychology program, we were able to use senior psychology students as experimenters for a year in return for independent study academic credit. Our typical group consisted of four to six seniors each year (some staying for more than one year), who met once weekly throughout the year for instruction at first and data presentation and interpretation later; and each year, after we had learned to work together, we found the experience highly collaborative, even intense. Each new participant was interesting and we became fascinated by the questions his or her image evoked and by the personality that emerged. Such work produced enthusiasm and in many cases a dedication to the project, and I wish to thank again all those whose work was good and above all those whose work rose to the highest levels.

The image makers were for the most part undergraduates as well, of about twenty years of age, although a few were older. Almost all were recruited from art or psychology classes, roughly in equal proportions, but a few were acquaintances of one or another experimenter; we were not always sure that this was a good idea in view of the intimate material that would be shared, but we discussed it with each other and with the potential participant beforehand and minimized the intrusion and exposure. In retrospect, I am happy to have taken the risk, since some of the people in their thirties or early forties turned out to be the most fascinating.

A word needs to be said about the complex motivations of our image makers. Some, of course, needed experimental credit in the

---

[1] The time was brief when compared to an ideal, but it was still quite long: typically we worked with each individual for about eight hours.

classes they were taking. But all seemed motivated above all by a desire for self-knowledge—at least to observe themselves at work with a new instrument and perhaps take advantage of our offer to give them our individual interpretation. To those who came in for this we would explain how we viewed the relation between their personality and their image making, and ask for their comments. These in turn became a new kind of datum: a check on the plausibility of our clinical think-ing, or a stimulus to further development of the interpretation.

GROUPING THE PARTICIPANTS: CLUSTER ANALYSIS

Over five years we studied 72 image makers, and accumulated that many individual interpretations. From one point of view they were perfectly satisfactory; they seemed plausible and meaningful. From another point of view they were limited, because they communicated only the individual richness of approaches to art, but no sense of order or commonality. We now faced two possible kinds of analysis which would bridge the individual particularities: one which would attempt to correlate various aspects of the images with various aspects of the personalities, and another which would search for groupings of image makers distinguishable by their mode of work.

The analysis one chooses to perform reveals one's assumptions about causality and about the interconnections of data. I wish to make mine explicit. I rejected a correlational analysis because when it is used to explain a phenomenon it assumes a regular relation between causes and effects—for example, more of cause C causing more of an effect E. There seems no reason to base one's analysis on such a model; even if the cause-effect vocabulary were to be appropriate, an effect (say, denseness of composition) might have more than one cause (say, obses-siveness in cognitive style, or presence of a broad and pervasive danger to be mastered). It seems better to group one's effects and ascertain what causes explain them. They may vary somewhat, but they will also have something in common; and what they have in common will become the core of our explanation, with the rest hopefully fitting into a pattern.

The procedure used for grouping the effects—the process and end product of image making—without imposing artificial dimensions on them was cluster analysis. We first rated each image, and the process by which it was made, on a large number of distinguishable and recurrent characteristics (there were 21; see Appendix B, "Image and Process Assessment"); this was done by three groups of two raters working independently, who then discussed their differences with the encouragement to resolve them. In practice, what resulted were some adjustments of scores in response to this, but no attempts at complete agreement. Even so, the interrater agreements were satisfactory, with the intra-class rs ranging from .85 to .97. The 21 mean ratings were then factor analyzed to reduce them to a much smaller number of orthogonal dimensions. Five dimensions resulted: we called them image-based narrative, timidity, flowing process, formality, and expansiveness (Appendix B, Table 1). These were compact enough to submit to a cluster analysis.

A cluster analysis gives one a range of solutions rather than a single solution, and one must choose the one that best responds to one's purpose. At one end there is the most general solution—two clusters— while at the other there is an increasingly large number of smaller and smaller clusters. It seemed preferable to opt for the finest subdivision, as long as it retained coherence; this meant retaining all clusters that had more than five members (five being the number of factors used in the analysis). This gave us a seven-cluster solution.

Appendix B also lists the contribution of each factor to the definition of each cluster (Table 2) and presents a discriminant analysis which describes each image maker's relation to his or her cluster (Tables 3 through 9). This consists of the individual factor scores obtained by each person within each cluster, and the correlation between each person's scores and the mean scores of the clusters. The latter score is particularly useful in judging whether an individual is squarely placed within the cluster or might also be assigned elsewhere.

THE PLAN OF THE BOOK

The next and certainly most crucial step was to see what consistency existed in the psychodynamics revealed within each cluster. We had prepared for this step, of course, when we had done the individual interpretations, and now we could see to what degree the interpretations were consistent within each cluster. I replicate this process in presenting the findings: for each cluster, I begin with a succinct summary of the dynamics of each participant, and build up to a statement of the dynamics of the group. (This process was in fact not simply inductive, but also reciprocal; certain variables might leap to the eye only when formulating the statement, and compel a second look. For example, what seemed in one cluster to be a common thread of wish-fulfillment, which was easy to see individually, was connected to a pattern of having severe or distant fathers, who had not seemed important at first. Now the connection between the two variables would become clear: the participants had all wished to come close to their fathers but could not. In the context of the group, and in contrast to other clusters, the fathers now loomed large, and helped explain the consistency of the cluster and the frustrations that exacerbated the wishes that still needed fulfilling.)

Following the general statement, I discuss two individuals at greater length; this serves to indicate my respect for the complexity of each life, and for the struggles to give it coherence, that the participants were kind enough to reveal to us.

The more one relies on the richness of one's clinical understanding, the more skeptical one must be of the tendency to see patterns where there may in fact be none. To satisfy myself on this score, I had an independent analysis done of the first four clusters to be analyzed (the first, fourth, sixth, and seventh clusters). In this analysis, two senior psychology undergraduates who knew nothing of my own analysis, Joseph Keiser and Kristoffer Berlin, were asked to study the personality data and look for any regularities they might find in it. Their analysis is presented in Appendix A, and the results are remarkably close to my own observations on these clusters. I am reassured by this analysis that the psychology underlying our image makers' work is real, and that we have not invented the patterns that we have seen.

CHAPTER 3

First Cluster

Narrative Informality and Compensatory Longings

The first cluster is exemplified by broad shapes and very little emphasis on form or composition; there is a certain up-beat mood to them, but very little idiosyncrasy or originality. So we may interpret the factor scores, which are, in descending order, "expansiveness", "informality", and "timidity" (see Table 3 in the Appendix). To a greater degree than any other cluster they also tell a story, and tell it broad strokes, as it were; none of the artists worked on their image under magnification. We may say that stylistically what they have is a certain narrative informality.[1]

Let us look at the images themselves (see Figs 8–15). *Estate*, for example, simply represents a seigneurial house isolated in a lush park; the image remains straightforward and narrative, but gone from the original are the little houses that had populated the middle of the original photograph, and gone are the swings—the only traces of children at play. *Highway Home* shows us a road made to jut abruptly into the landscape (and return from it), while *Saturn*, an image that builds on the same landscape, precariously suspends a representation of the planet above the land. In *Feeling through to the Flow of Water* five hands reach for the lush fruit while a cascade of blue water flows down on the left. The composition of *Life*, while seemingly abstract, is based on the six-petal star-gazer lily and three of the other flowers in our still life, and explicitly conveys a message of harmony between the races of

---

[1] The cluster is also quite homogeneous, in that none of the individuals could be assigned to any other cluster (Table 3b), and it is highly distinct from the others because no other cluster shares either the expansiveness or this degree of informality.

humankind. *Yee World*, an unusually happy picture, completely ignores the photograph on which it was superimposed, but instead tells the story of mythical creatures called "yees" populating a brightly colored landscape, barely disturbed by their one enemy, the "yip" at the top of the hill.

It is evident that none of the pictures emphasize composition; in some unstylized manner they seem to tell or imply a story. *Sunset*, barely changed from its original except for much blurring and a lurid sky, suggests a peculiar mood rather than a specific story, but the mood does not require any formal emphasis either. *Flying Peachy Buttheads* at first seems different, with the stylized elongation of its fruits, but it is in fact the accidental outcome of a planless mode of working rather than a willful portrayal, and it was rated as highly informal and expansive on that basis. What seems to set this cluster apart is that, in order to describe its images, we have to describe not their form but what is going on inside them.

It is this emphasis on content as against form that arrests our attention. Can we can speak of a predominant purpose and mode of working here, and if so, can we discern a mode of relating behind them? Proceeding inductively, from the original interpretations, and building up a picture of the cluster step by step, will reveal a simple, governing motive: *these painters are motivated by compensatory longings to produce a better reality than the one they had known.*

THE PSYCHOLOGICAL PROCESS SEEN INDIVIDUALLY

Recall that when the individual interpretations were made, we knew nothing about the clusters that might result or the ways in which these images might be interconnected. If the original interpretations turn out to be consistent, then we will have support for their validity; and we will be able to see the images as hanging together psychologically, not only by style of image and mode of working.

One can begin with any participant. The young man who painted **Estate**, for example, said after he had finished that he felt comfortable out in the woods, away from the big city, and that the house he had created was peaceful. "I feel like that's my house, like I could live there." When asked whether he would live alone, he replied, "Well, it's a pretty big house; you could invite a lot of people. But it's not in a big city; I mean the other people there would be people you know." Somewhat laconic and reserved in his answers, he nevertheless seems

Figure 8. Estate

Figure 9. Highway Home

Figure 10. Saturn

Figure 11. Life

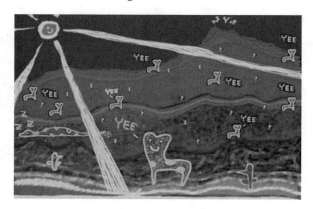

Figure 12. Yee World

Figure 13. Sunset

to make clear that the estate he has created represents a fulfillment of a dream. It is not a dream without its ambiguities, admittedly: at one point he said that his ideas had just changed, and when asked what that was about, he said, "just thinking that it might be unreasonable to set the village on fire. I mean I could, if I wanted to."

Our surprise at this revelation of anger was not explained until he appeared for the psychodynamic interview, in which he told us that what he most remembered about his father "has to do with me being punished or something." The father would bottle up his anger until it reached the explosive point, and this is something in which, to his regret, he resembles him now; in any event, he does not like his father at all. He has seen little of him since the parents were divorced (first when he was two and for the second time when he was seven), and although he made attempts later to get in touch with him, he finally decided that the father was going to remain unreachable. He wrote him a letter saying that he did not want him in his life any more; he adds that although the decision was right, he does feel the loss now. It is an emptiness that his mother, a good caretaker but an emotionally distant person as well, does not fill either. She is still angry at the father, and this reminds her of the constant fighting between the parents when he was small. There is a pessimistic cast to him, a lack of enthusiasm even for his present girl friend, with whom he fights over who is being adequately cared for. The image he created was of a better life, but it was not one that his anger or his depression could allow him really to enjoy.

Highway Home has a clear personal referent for the student who made it. Although at first he was concerned only with clarifying the structure of the landscape he had started with, he was soon reminded of the drive home from the university and decided to draw in the highway. Later, when asked if the image had meaning, he laughed and said, "I think that's the path of life, I guess. You're living on the cliff, you're on the danger zone going back and forth … . And as you can see, on the left side, there is nothing but a cliff … . And you can talk about life and how if you take the wrong path, then you're doomed." But his tone is neither anxious nor pessimistic, merely determined.

The son of supportive parents—he saw his father as powerful, influential, and wise, and the mother as caring and emotionally close—he nevertheless remembered his childhood as far from safe. His family had been comfortable and wealthy in their native Viet Nam but had to leave it abruptly; their separations, their escape, their encounters with pirates, their three-year wait to come to the US, and their having to start from zero—from a "clean slate"—are well remembered and very much part of his and his family's present identity. With hard work and mutual support the parents have become reasonably comfortable now and certainly are working toward the betterment of their children, and the children all wish to get an education, succeed, and be able to return something for the sacrifices that the family has made for them. His own determination seems as matter-of-fact to us as his subordination of personal impulse to long-term goals seems natural to him. The image he had created does represent a kind of wish for the return of a better life but it also reveals the second start in life—the clean slate—and the present attempts to master dangers of which he is only too aware. It is a narrative that represents a resolve.

The young woman who painted **Saturn** intended originally to change the midday scene into Greece at sunset, with a white surrealistic moon hanging in the sky. She spent much time coloring the sky dark blue and purple, then produced a moon that was not altogether satisfactory to her and so added a ring to it to make Saturn; she also transformed the texture of the landscape by using several filters. When done, she said that she liked the "clean cuteness of the planet", and when asked later about the image's possible relation to her life said, "that's interesting, maybe the alien aspect to everything—feeling alienated in some forms of life." The daughter of a self-centered, stubborn, emotionally distant and prejudiced father, she resembles him a bit in her aggressiveness and competitiveness, but is closer to her mother, who was always warm and caretaking, and resembles her in her own sensitivity to others. The intellect she has inherited from her father leaves her feeling guilty for having transcended her mother's limitations.

Her childhood has, however, left a bitter taste in her mouth because it was spent in the fundamentalist American South, to which she hopes never to return. She also recalls that she had always felt alienated from her family, as if there were something wrong with her (unlike her sister, who never questioned anything and never did anything wrong), and we may suppose that the constricting society she remembers also stands for her family. Because she also came in for a debriefing session at the conclusion of our testing, we were able to ask whether the planet might not be an image of herself, and she agreed that it well might; she added that the way it hangs in space suggests that she has been left in an uncertain spot (she remembered that she had told us earlier that the planet looked like it was ready to crash into the ground). Yes, the image was in a way an idealized self-portrait—in which, we might add, the clean idealization of herself is closely allied with her vivid memory of childhood alienation and constraints.

The unusually frank and open young man who painted **Feeling Through to the Flow of Water** (Fig. 14) knew right away that the image had an intense personal referent. Focusing on the persimmon fruit of the original Leaves photograph, he isolated the section that contained it, drew five hands reaching for it using his own hands and those of the woman experimenter as models, and then drew the water and the rocks it flowed through. He made clear to us right after he completed the image that he was identified strongly with his mother, an affectionate— even crazy, undisciplined, certainly artistic—woman with four children by as many fathers. He seems to have been her favorite and the only consistent male in her life, and certainly remains close to her now; going to college was his first real separation from her (although he remembers other separations when she would run off with some of the fathers of her other children). He also remembers vividly his separation from his father when he was three years old.

When he was sixteen, he searched for and found his father in another state, but the father was neither interested in him nor receptive to a meeting, and his new wife was jealous of the slightest possible relationship between them. He withdrew, disappointed, made another attempt by sending him a graduation announcement, but that was returned, and he gave up altogether. The biggest void in his life is, as he puts it, his male energy, but on the other hand his mother has always been the ultimate female. Even that closeness was not enough to protect him from a pervasive feeling of loss, however, and we need not search far for the meaning of his image: it represents a yearning for the lost parents, the one always distant and now withdrawn forever, the other close but disappearing whenever she needed to. It is a remarkable image; alone in this cluster it does not sacrifice aesthetic coherence for its narrative needs. Both its richness and the wealth of information the subject gives us about himself invite a closer look at him later in this chapter.

The picture **Life** returns us to a world of pure narrative symbolism, however. Designed from the start to isolate the flowers of the original still life by simplifying the background, it seemed to progress by a series of suppressions; once the flowers were isolated, they could be painted over if their colors were unappealing. The central lily is rendered in six colors, receives a subtle cross on one of its petals, and the vase is rendered in grey with a private symbol in mustard superimposed on it. The young man who painted the picture is aware of much of his symbolism ("every one of these colors represents something when you give a rose to somebody"), and allows us to deduce the rest. Yes, the picture represents life: the colors of the lily represent the wished for harmony between the races of mankind, the cross represents salvation through God, the vase is society, and the private symbol his own "signature on the society". Purple and pink, in general, represent sin, while pinkish yellow represents goodness and helpfulness. He adds that he had chosen the still life to work on because the last girl he had been interested in liked flowers.

The son of a strict father who died when the subject was a boy, and a protector mother who took over and worked hard to keep the family together, he was diagnosed with leukemia while still in high school and his life has been dominated by it since then. He went through the cumbersome and painful treatments; formerly an atheist, he became a born-again Christian. His life has taken on a very determined cast: beside fighting his illness, he has become less selfish and more open to others, and wants to repay some of the help he had received during his illness by becoming a hospital counselor. With his conversion, it is as if everything has taken on a symbolic meaning, sometimes through public symbols, at other times private ones. The harmony he would like to see between the races is not without its personal referent either; he did tell us that he has discussed interracial dating with his mother and that she replied, "well, if you're happy, it's your choice." The very decision to work on flowers seems to represent that situation: the girl who liked them is probably the one he had discussed with his mother, and we discover in later conversation that she had recently rejected him. Thus both resolve and loss animate his picture making.

The bright, sprightly, childlike **Yee World** hides a complex personal history. When the subject came in for his interview, a few days after completing his image, he told the interviewer, "I was just thinking on the way up, if there are questions about my parents, it's a volatile question. I am angry at them." He was, indeed: at his father for not listening, for being insecure, and for having a violent temper, and at his mother for being irrational, dominating, unstable, and judgmental. They divorced when he was young, but from his point of view that only stopped their constant fighting. He respects neither of them, nor his step-parents, and when asked which one he identifies with he simply says, "neither; they serve as negative examples." He was afraid of both of them as a child.

He got into the habit early of going out of his way to make things all right for his mother—buying her gifts—just to keep her in a reasonably positive mood. He recalls having taken on the role of counselor to both parents and deciding later that he had to stop it. Still later he started to write plays and screen plays, and has had some public success with them. We see in these two ways of handling an admittedly disturbing and chaotic childhood the beginnings of an explanation of his happy image. He does serve as a kind of protector to others, and focuses on children now, particularly children of parents with AIDS. He writes and illustrates happy stories for them about a Yee World, in which the good Yees are protected against the bad Yips and the occasional Chomper by the benign Spotted Dragon (also seen in his image, sleeping). When asked if any part of this world was symbolic of him, he said that the Yees were. Thus, by the power of wishes, does he transform a dreary childhood, one that a more compliant child might wish to be forgotten, into a picture of a secure and happy land—for himself and others.

All of the six subjects we have looked at have made images which represented mastery over an unpleasant or dangerous reality. The mastery might be willful or dreamy—an affirmation or a poetic fulfillment— but it was in each case a reaction to a deficit or a loss. But the young woman who painted *Sunset* seems neither to have had a disappointing childhood nor to show any compensatory wishes in her image. (And her image is neither as "expansive" nor as "informal" as the others in this cluster.) Her transformations of the original Village photograph are more moody than wishful; she does not so much impose her needs on it as work closely with it. Spending most of her time on the exact shade the sky should be, she also blurs the image four times, and then adds a few points of light into the windows. We never came to understand the picture's mood, but did find out that the smudging is a characteristic of her photographic work: she says that she likes to blur her photographs, "especially the structures."

Her interview reveals hints of blurring as a cognitive style. Like her father, she does not like to read the instructions on anything and winds up doing things wrong, but like her mother, she is a meticulous housekeeper (although she likes to keep a mess in the invisible, private spaces); this seems to her an unresolved paradox. Her parents have always been close to her (with her mother seemingly ready to satisfy her every wish) and to each other, and are only now finding their own space apart from each other. Above all, she is not clear what her mother's role is: "half the time she acts as my mother and the other half we are like sisters; when I was younger, we used to pick on each other and tease each other." Perhaps it is this experience of unclear roles that she translates into the vagueness of description and personal goals that mark her interview—and perhaps it is cognitive style, rather than psychodynamic needs, that makes its way into the image.

With *Flying Peachy Buttheads* (Fig. 15) we return again to the primacy of personal needs. Focused from the start on the central persimmon—or peach, as it is commonly seen—the subject copies it several times, skews it and stretches it and distributes it throughout the frame, and then returns to the center to enlarge the undistorted original; at the end, she pastes four leaves onto it, two to serve as eyes, two as ears. Such central images tend to be projections of the artist—as with *Saturn* in this cluster—but exactly what is being projected here is never made clear.

Nevertheless, the subject gives us sufficient hints. She is the daughter of an intense, controlling, and intrusive, body-oriented psychotherapist father, with whom she did a lot of drawing as a child, and of a passionate, and equally controlling and intrusive, mother. Growing up with him was very intense, but she learned early to channel her own intensity into artistic expression. That expression is unfettered by control or thought or an aesthetic program: she just goes by the way things feel to her and stops when they look right. What becomes expressed in this image has an aggressive charge that we have seen seldom, at least in the frank form of distortions and dynamic movement it takes here; where we have seen it in other images it seemed informed by resentment and anger. In her frank, passionate and aggressive expression she may embody her father's therapeutic ideal. She is, in any case, sufficiently complex to suggest a much closer look.

THE PSYCHOLOGICAL DYNAMICS OF THIS CLUSTER

Both the informal style and emphasis on substance of six of the images can be explained by a *resolve* or *wish* to produce a better reality than the subjects had known. The childhoods of some were unusually constricting, of others marked by loss, of still others marked by both loss and illness; either a resolve to do better or a wish to have something better motivates all six.

The resolve or wish finds its way not only into their artistic expression but into plans for their life. One of the facts that stands out about this cluster is, as it were, actuarial, because it did not strike us when we attended only to the subjects' dynamics: all six of them want either to become therapists or do good for others.[2] Because they turn their wishes toward others, *their motives are as reparative as they are wish-fulfilling* and seem to produce the affirmative expansiveness that defined this cluster. *The primacy of these motives, and the practical*

[2] This was pointed out by Keiser and Berlin when they analyzed these data independently. See Chapter 10.

orientation of the artists, seems to overwhelm any desire, had their been one, for more formally conceived compositions.

Two subjects—*Sunset* and *Flying Peachy Buttheads*—work somewhat differently. The first, we have seen, does not really produce an image that belongs with the cluster, because it is neither as expansive nor as informal. The second, however, does belong, but her informality is seemingly not reparative, but rather angry and intense; its expression in the image is the consequence of uninhibited flow.

In order to flesh out the close interconnections between our subjects' psychodynamics and the images they make I shall describe two of them more fully. One is placed squarely in the center of this cluster, as it were, by virtue of the strength of his longings, while the other is more at the periphery by virtue of her bluntness. The one—*Feeling Through*—will illuminate what is typical here, while *Flying Peachy* will tell us how far the psychological process representing "informality" and "expansiveness" stretches. By attempting to understand each of them better, I hope to account for the range of motives that are at work here.

FEELING THROUGH TO THE FLOW OF WATER

We said that Van, as we shall call him, worked purposefully from the start. Quickly and imaginatively, he isolated the part of the Leaves photograph in the upper right that he wanted to work on and gave what remained a smooth, dull-green background. He integrated the two parts by a bit of smudging at the edges, and with what he had in front of him soon visualized hands reaching for the fruit. Now, using both his hands and those of the experimenter as models, he drew five closely intertwined hands reaching for the persimmon. In retrospect we might say that he had now given expression to his wish. What remained for him to do was an aesthetic matter: to fill in the blank left side. He decided to draw grey rocks right next to two of the arms and then the other rocks and the waterfall between them. The result is—unusually for this cluster—both aesthetic and deeply meaningful, and we shall see that the waterfall is part of that meaning.

Some of what we needed to know came up right after the image was finished when we asked our standard post-image questions. He mentioned the hands, the fruit, and the water, and said that they "grab your attention and pull you in." Soon after, he spoke of his mother—about whom we were to hear more than about anyone else—and said that she

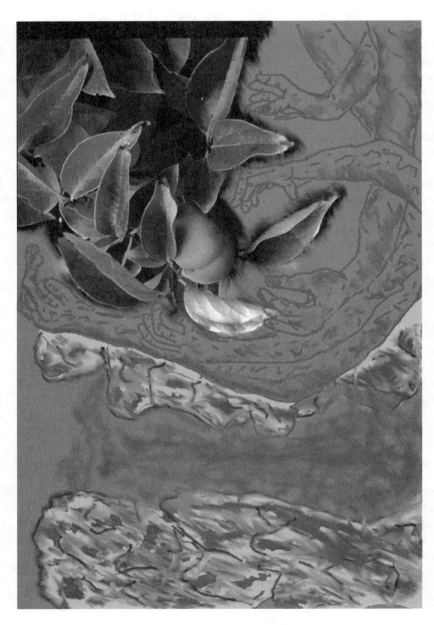

Figure 14. Feeling Through to the Flow of Water (Hands)

was a single mom who had raised him, his older brother, and two younger sisters. He seemed pleased that he had been her favorite, and noted that he identified with her closely; in many ways he wished men could bear children, and knew that they had to console themselves by creating art. He also told us something about his father, with whom he attempted to build a relationship, but who refused. We should emphasize that he said all of this without any specific questions or prods; the focus of this brief interview was on the image making itself. He then told us something about the waterfall. It illustrated a recent experience he had had at an actual waterfall, when, alone, he was approached by two owls; inspired, he quickly wrote a song, one of whose lines was, "Hoo, hoo, where is my Mom, hoo, hoo, I love my Mom."

In his frank way he put his attachment to his mother and his feminine identification forward, and helped explain the content of both parts of the image immediately. Later, in the psychodynamic interview, we asked him about some of these themes more systematically. His mother is an artist with a master's degree who has taught art classes but for now prefers to take care of Van's youngest sister. Painting big canvases—"really, she paints her life"—she is serious about her work and tries to sell it. "My Mom is great, she is kind of the crazy artist, she's not logical in a lot of ways, but her energy toward life really shows and her love for children is really there … . She's the kind of mom that will always love her children, no matter what they do, and I guess that I learned love from her … . She is very instinctual, very feeling, whereas I am the thinking kind of person."

Asked to give us some memories of her when he was younger, he said, "She was very motherly, she would take care of me, she was very attentive—I was breastfed till, like, three years—she didn't want to see me hurt or cry, and she always placed me first." But any memory of such closeness is invariably attached to a memory of separation, and Van's is no exception: "She sent me off to summer camp, and I was only seven years old, and I totally freaked out. It was because she had had an operation and she was seeing this guy, and she drank a bit too much in that part of her life, and so there was some neglect there."

His father left when he was three, as we said, and it is not difficult to imagine the pain of the simultaneous loss of the breast and the father; and Van has many other memories of separations. Her four children have four fathers, and "I used to hold it against my mom to a certain extent, but, you know, she shared the experience of each one and I really understood that she wasn't the one that was at fault. These men just weren't capable of intimacy. I guess I really freaked out when it came down to the fact that they had wives and children." Indeed, he recalls vividly a story he was told of his brother walking with his mother and seeing one of the fathers coming down the street with his pregnant wife. "My mom said, 'I am not going to be a fool anymore,' and ran off to Paris or something."

For all the closeness to his mother there was then the ineluctable pain of separation. With his father there was, it would seem, only separation: he remembers beating on the screen door, crying, knowing that the father was leaving for the last time because he could hear himself saying, "I won't see you again." When Van looked him up half-way across the continent at the age of sixteen, "he just wasn't receptive at all; his wife said, 'You can't have a relationship with him or else I'll divorce you'." When, much later, his graduation announcement was returned to him, he knew that the only thing to do was to let the father go.

He resembles his mother in making the most of a precarious economic situation, and his father in being a tinkerer, but what seems most important for understanding him is the strength of his wishes and goals. They are primarily emotional. "I have a goal that has to do with my family. I envision myself having a family, out in the woods outside of society, … where I would have really close friends and we could all live in close proximity and raise each other's kids … . I want to be a therapist, I value a career, but family is at the top of the pyramid."

Van's recognition of his needs and feelings, and of his reaching out for a male model, is as remarkable as their strength itself. In his image he reaches for his mother both as fruit and as waterfall (not without competition from siblings), and perhaps more broadly he reaches out toward a lost father and the maleness he feels is missing in him. He makes the needs satisfied by his image making crystal clear, and leaves us only to wonder how the image became as coherent and as aesthetic as it did. But neither he nor we have an answer to that question.

FLYING PEACHY BUTTHEADS

The woman I call Sarah is the daughter of two intense and controlling parents. She takes on some of those qualities: her own intensity is suggested by her image, and her need for control is seen in her interview. Focused on the "peach" from the start, she seemed to connect immediately with this sensuous and suggestive object, but whether because she felt identified with it or was choosing it as an object of attachment is impossible to say. She made it violet, then made several copies of it and scattered them throughout the picture. She then skewed and stretched them, erased some of them and turned the remaining ones back into orange. She went on to change the color of some of the leaves, turn them back to the original, and begin to paint the background a uniform color in order to simplify the composition. She chose brown at first (and the experimenter, noting that she was wearing all brown, asked if there was a connection, a question she dismissed by saying that it was rust, not brown) and then changed it to a dark blue-green.

Returning to the central fruit she enlarged it, found a small green leaf in the picture, copied it twice and pasted the copies onto it. Adding the little points that she came to call ears, she then added similar points to some of the stretched peaches that were left. She seemed amused by her work, and somewhat teasing: after adding the points to one of the stretched peaches she looked over her shoulder as if to say, "those are not banana slugs (the university mascot) as you thought, but something flying." Smearing some dark brown on the central fruit, she made and stretched a few more copies and was done.

Sarah claimed afterwards that she had had no plan, but did like the way the peaches were looking; after simplifying the background, she started to see them as flying, and although that represented a change of direction, it was worth adhering to. Explaining the absence of a plan, she says, "creating art is a whole personal process, just the way you feel when you are doing it", just as going to museums is for her a matter of relating to something, something that may trigger some sort of emotion. She adds that she has "always been in art. Finger painting, sculpture ... I used to do art with my father, drawing pictures together, and we would also explore creative birds together, drawing creative things." (An anthropology major, she decided to minor in art and got her first formal exposure to it there.) She is considering doing art therapy because art is an important means of expression, while language is easily misinterpreted or inadequate to say what one wanted to say. Returning to the image, Sarah says that she likes it because "it has an antagonist, ... and the leaves and the background color all tie in together." Perhaps the choice of "antagonist" for the more appropriate "protagonist" is not accidental. In any case, at the end she agrees to give the image a title, and says, "it kind of looks to me—but I didn't intend this—like flying peachy buttheads", and laughs.

Several weeks later, in the dynamic interview, she was open, frank, focused, and quite brief in her answers. The interviewer summarized his impressions by writing, "She seemed calm and relaxed. She was friendly and cooperative. She maintained the interview at a very intellectual level and was very amicable ... . I also felt that she took herself

Figure 15. Flying Peachy Buttheads

very seriously and that she has a strong sense of entitlement. At certain times she seemed condescending, and somewhat annoyed at me. I also felt that she was in total control of the interview. She was skillful at avoiding answering certain questions."

One of two siblings in an intense and, one might conclude, provocative household, Sarah is the daughter of a body-oriented psychotherapist and a capable woman who has held a number of jobs in business, traveled abroad, and done much volunteer work. They were divorced when she was five. Describing her father when she was young, she says, "When I was younger I didn't really understand him. I wanted to have a normal father, or what I considered a normal father. I've always been close to my father but I always thought he was kind of out there. I would be embarrassed to bring my friends to meet him. He is a very deep person and he won't communicate with you at a frivolous level. He doesn't chitter chatter. When you're younger and you have your friends coming over and he's asking them what the meaning of life is ... very deep questions, very stimulating. But when you're a child, you don't want a stimulating father. I don't know what you want as a kid. I was embarrassed to bring my friends because none of them could understand him. And then later on in life, the things that he said to me when I was younger, like philosophy, would make sense." Asked for an example, she adds, "he would say there is no such things as accidents. At the time, I would think, 'Of course there are accidents: I dropped my milk, so what?' And now I believe him. There aren't any accidents. He would tell me, 'You don't know yourself.' I would say, 'Of course, I know myself; I am ten years old.' "

Such a childhood may seem overstimulating and ill tuned to the needs of the child, but one has the impression that Sarah's excellent memory and undaunted intellect have proved capable of dealing with it. She can certainly accept, now, that she resembles him in certain ways: they are alike, she says, in their ways of understanding people, and by that she means "picking up on people's insecurities and fears. I am just very in tune with people's energy. We are both pretty creative. He's not an artist or anything, but he's got a creative mind, like for poetry. He's a good listener. He's stubborn, I'm stubborn. We both like to argue." She adds that they both like to push people's buttons, but that he does it a lot more. "He can be pretty stimulating; it can be very uncomfortable sometimes ... . He wants to get people excited. He likes to see the excitement. He likes to see people in touch with their inner emotions ... . He likes the power."

To this picture of an intrusive father, whom she now understands and accepts, one must add the intense and controlling mother. Where her father has taught her about "the inner stuff", her mother has taught her a lot about different cultures, taking the children to live in Mexico and Indonesia. "She's more worldly; she's into exploring different cultures—she's exciting that way." Asked if she could say more about what "exciting" means in her mother's case, Sarah gives us an answer that betrays some ambivalence: "I envy her; she just does whatever she wants to do. She does what makes her happy. She's very passionate, very in tune with her Id. She very much likes to please—she very much likes pleasure. She does whatever she wants; everything is possible for her. She's very driven: if she wants something, she's going to get it." Both her parents are controlling, she adds, and her mother is very persuasive. And like her mother, Sarah is driven, and believes that she can do whatever she wants to do (although she wishes she could be as pleasure oriented).

Let us look at Sarah's image again. It is obviously not an image of wish, resolution, or reparation. It is informal and "expansive", but in ways that differ considerably from the others in the cluster. She is admittedly in the center of things (as the enlarged peach), and there is a sensuous and perhaps scatological cast to the self-representation (in the *butthead* title, in smearing some dark brown on the peach, and in choosing brown for the first background). But its informality seems more the product of a dynamic mode of feeling and working, a frankness and even bluntness of dealing with oneself and others, rather than of a compensatory wish. (Indeed, such wishes can be seen in retrospect but they did not strike us as important then, so we do not wish to emphasize them unduly now. Her father was emotionally close but she used to wish for a normal one; perhaps her present identification with his directness and his ability to "pick up on people's insecurities" is a way of bringing him back closer to her.) Perhaps one can feel some of her mother's intensity, or her father's insistence on the primacy of one's innermost feelings, in the dynamic diagonals—and the very stretch— of the distorted fruits and in the frank complementary contrast of the orange with the blue-green.

It seems natural for Sarah to wish to let up. She can agree with her father that she should do whatever makes her happy, and do it without being driven. "I don't want the pressure to have to write papers by a certain time. I want to be able to play, to paint, and draw, and have fun, and explore different things. I want to be able to go to exhibits without the pressure, … I want to read a book because I want to read a book … . I don't want to *be* an artist … . In terms of art, I want time to explore various things, to be able to play with it."

In this cluster, then, an informal style and the presence of a satisfying fantasy are connected to a *resolve* or *wish* to construct a better reality than one the subjects had known; their childhoods were unusually constricting, or marked by loss, or by both loss and illness. The wishes might be called reparative, and their primacy overshadows any need for composition. Such is the case with six subjects.

Two subjects are somewhat different. The image of one (*Sunset*) does not quite fit the cluster, nor does her history or personality, and need not detain us. But the other, *Flying Peachy Buttheads*, is informal and expansive like the other images, yet is more the product of a style, of a dynamic frankness and bluntness. Compensatory wishes may be the characteristic determinants of informality and expansiveness, but the style can be achieved in other ways.

CHAPTER 4

Second Cluster

Inhibited, Disconnected Forms
and Downcast, Angry Lives

This cluster, like the last one, consists of informally organized images, but they are constrictive where the previous ones were expansive; that is to say that their mood is dampened and their visual language small-scaled rather than broad. In the last cluster the affirmative expansiveness and the informality both seemed to be the consequence of the wish-fulfilling and reparative needs that animated the painters; their motives seemed to crowd out any desire for more formally conceived compositions. Do similar motives crowd out form here as well?

For them to do so, this cluster would have to be a mirror image of the last one, and while this may be the case for the prevalent mood, which here is negative, it is not the case for the other dimensions. Here we have no story being told, no narrative being represented. The images are merely loosely organized; their informality is not at the service of story-telling but rather the consequence of a disconnected mode of dealing with the image. We shall see that much of the looseness mirrors the disconnection that the participants feel with others, which in turn is connected with their need to manage considerable anger; there is much loss, pain, or disappointment, here, too, but no reparative balance.

This is a large cluster—perhaps because it is less sharply defined than most of the others—and it will be easier to follow the individual dynamics if they are grouped by the image which was their starting point. Here, the starting point seems to have an intimate connection with the end point, with the Flower picture inviting a certain avoidant daintiness, and the Village picture inviting a representation of family mood, as we shall see in later chapters as well. With those constraints, a downcast landscape may turn out somewhat differently from an equally downcast still life. But all the original pictures except for Hillside seemed capable of being drawn into our painters' inhibited, ill-defined process.

THE PSYCHOLOGICAL PROCESS SEEN INDIVIDUALLY

The Flower Pictures

The young woman who produced *Mosaic Flowers* told us when she had finished that the only art she does is with children; she does finger painting with them, and because it won't do to have your pictures looking better than theirs, "you just smear things around". If this minimizes the role of intention in making images with finger paints, it also captures her approach to this one. Having come to the study from a wish to help me when I asked for volunteers, she works willingly but without being quite sure where she wants to go. She magnifies one flower after another, works on a small part of it, then brings it back down to size; she outlines one or another flower and imposes a filter on it; at the end—except for outlining the narcissus with another filter—she imposes the mosaic filter repeatedly on most of the rest of the image, and achieves the patterned effect we see. At no point does she "touch" the image with a brush or pencil.

Figure 16. Mosaic Flowers

Figure 17. Filtered Flowers

Figure 18. Tapestry

Figure 19. Mosaic Sky

Figure 20. Society

Figure 21. Goya

Figure 22. Smudgie-Pie

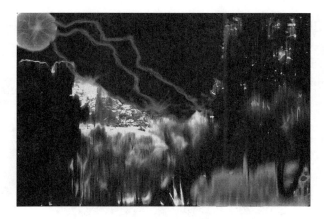

Figure 23. Lightning

Figure 24. Growing

Figure 25. Tears

Figure 26. Reflections

Figure 27. Monster

The daughter of a quarrelsome couple, she had withdrawn into her own world as a child. The household was not merely quarrelsome: it was informed by an ugly and to her a painful secret which everyone conspired to keep swept under the rug: her father had had a girl friend during most of the years of the marriage, complete with a baby and another house, which everyone in a way knew about but no one admitted.

The father is an angry man who to this day does not admit that any of this had happened, while the mother, who had lived in a glass bubble most of her life, has kicked her husband out to protect the daughter against his anger. Now free and adventuresome, the mother has a boyfriend and travels about the country with him. But the daughter has paid a price for all this, having begun to feel guilty about surpassing her mother, and having been diagnosed as depressed and in need medication in order to function. And though she dislikes her father, she fears she is like him in the depth of her anger; until the 7th grade she had been a bully in school, but then changed abruptly and became depressed. (She is also somewhat like her mother in having allowed herself to be duped by an outrageously dishonest boyfriend.) Happily, an identification with a friend's healthy mother, with whom she has always spent a lot of time, gives her present relationship a healthier cast, and her future a certain amount of hope.

Her distant relation to her image seems as much a mirror of her suppression of emotion and the family's denial of painful knowledge, as her lack of organization is a reflection of a relentless underpinning of contained anger.

Filtered Flowers—a title barely different from the previous one— is an image constructed in much the same way: it is transformed solely by filters, with one transformation following another without plan, and in its minute, pixel-by-pixel corrections of mistakes it is even more cautious. The young woman who had constructed it is said by her interviewer to be very unrevealing, and we come to understand why that should be so. The daughter of a man who abandoned the mother before she was born, she was raised by a distant, controlling and narrow-minded stepfather and by a mother whom she says she idolized; this she no longer does, but she cannot describe her in any other than ideal terms. She has no memories of her parents from her early childhood, but she does recall that a little later she and her half-brother both feared the mother because she was the one to discipline them (with a belt). She had been her stepfather's "little girl", but now that he too has left the family, she feels abandoned by him, and yet is no closer to her mother: her mother shows no interest in her present circumstances at all.

Her upbringing was nevertheless fundamentalist, at one point in the Catholic Church and at another in the Mormon Church, but she broke away from both with considerable anger. She is still a very angry person; when she gets angry, "I just totally go off and vent it all the way." When working with us her voice ranges from the flat and quiet, as if to protect herself against pain, to the explosive. After her parents separated she became religious again and knows that she did so to replace her family. We might be tempted to suggest that this helps contain her anger, too; anger, in any case, is an intimate part of her relationship with her boyfriend because, unlike the woman who produced *Mosaic Flowers*, she is highly sexual, but uses sexuality only for the discharge of stress, tension, and anger; indeed, and for similar reasons, "sex and religion are where my interests lie".

Perhaps the history she has revealed illuminates something about the nature of form. Beside the avoidant, hands-off use of filters, her image reveals no connections between things; it is as if the tenuous bonds by which she relates to others were pictured here abstractly. She does say, "I am a very solitary person; I try not to need anything from friends", and does add, "I've had enough pain for one lifetime."

We remain with the use of filters, and with cautiousness and uncertainty, with the young woman who produced **Tapestry**. Like the preceding woman, she makes her corrections pixel by pixel; unlike her, she turns to the Photoshop manual for ideas on how to proceed. Except for an occasional use of the pencil to emphasize boundaries, and the Smudge tool to make them realistic, she prefers "to have the computer do it for me". If the reader wonders why the image she produced does not fit its title, it is because she went back to the third of her eight saved images: the eighth one was indeed so heavily filtered and so monochromatic that "tapestry" was the best title for it, but she became worried about the degree of abstraction she had reached and returned to this earlier, safer, more realistic version, and kept the title.

She, too, is the daughter of an ultimately distant man; he connected with her only by joking around. Nevertheless, she, too was "daddy's little girl", though she knows now that he was dependent on her, and she knows it because now that she is out of the house she protects him by telling him that she had never really left him. Her mother was also—like the previous one—the punisher in the family, although she was also open and expressive, and the daughter remembers that they always fought a lot. "I didn't let people step on me, ... so when I thought my parents weren't treating me fairly I would ... voice it and tell them ... and it would turn into a big fight instead of just a discussion, ... I would be yelling at them and then they'd ground me for being a smartass, but after a couple of days I could just go to my dad and hug and just say, 'please, please', and I was off."

All of this rebelliousness came to an abrupt end. When she was in high school her parents were involved in a car accident and nearly died; she had to take care of them and they became more like her children. Having become the parent, she started to appreciate them; in fact, she apologized to them for how bad a child she had been. The parents, having more or less recovered, are now dependent on each other and neither one can leave the other though they might have wished it earlier; they are held together by their incapacity.

Asked about her goals in life, our artist says something revealing: she has become interested in relationships between couples, and thinks that she may become a family and/or sex therapist. We believe that this reveals something else, this time about her aesthetic form: the elements of her image hold together no better than those of the first two.

The Village Pictures

It is quite possible that the Flower picture invites episodic treatment by its incoherent structure; it is a photograph whose purpose seems to be to show the widest variety of color reproducible on the computer, and there seems no obvious way to integrate it without imposing an artificial structure upon it. But our present group, though working with a unified photograph with clear tensions between the upper and middle part, shows the episodic approach, too, though it is visible more in their manner of working than in the product.

The painter of **Mosaic Sky** is, indeed, a painter in the more narrow sense; she is one of the only two art majors in this group. She does bring her experiences in painting class to the task at hand: she wishes to work with shapes, colors, and space, as in the abstract painting her class is working with, and wishes to follow the preferred procedure, which is to "let it do what it will do and then respond to what is happening instead of trying to control it tightly." We cannot, then, ascribe an undirected process entirely to her, although we may presume that she finds it congenial. Her initial stated purpose is to accentuate the distinctions between light and dark, but she spends most of her time sharpening textures with the appropriate filters and retouching individual objects under magnification; she is never anything other than frustrated, "scattered and unsure", as the tester notes. The dark sky seems too emphatic, too ill-fitting.

Her relation to her parents was quite different from that of the first three women we have looked at. The daughter of a supportive, involved father and mother—the one a medical doctor and the other working in an office—she has somewhat the opposite problem: after their divorce, the relationship with her father became too close and that with her mother, strained. It was the father who was "inappropriately emotionally intimate," and it was only after becoming a Christian that he found appropriate boundaries; the daughter, likewise, became a Christian shortly afterward, and their relationship became one where each could love the other. Her mother has never taken emotional risks, a point in which she resembles her, and, like her, is a people pleaser; both parents, in their own way, seem dependent on the daughter.

Nevertheless, her newly found religion gives her the controls and meaning that she needs. When the parents separated, while she was in high school, she began praying and found that the next day she was overwhelmed by images of the cross, and, as she puts it, she made her choice, and her conviction has only deepened since then. She puts her goals into religious terms: to know God better and perhaps in the long run to pastor people.

Her sense of wholeness, we may say, comes from the outside, and the integration of her image is minimal at best; her interventions, too, are minimal and reflect little of the freedom that her painting class encourages. Her image takes no more visual risks than she does emotional ones. Is there a more vulnerable core to which this darkness—or the intended contrast between light and dark—might correspond? She herself provides a couple of suggestive observations. Her friendships emphasize a commitment to reconciliation, and love and safety in being who we are with all our problems; this suggests a glimpse of something we had not been able to see directly before. And her prominent fear is this: "that someday I am going to get married and then this person I'm going to marry is going to die within five years and I'm going to be widowed."

Darkness is not a mere metaphor but a pervasive reality in another version of the Village picture entitled *Society*. The title was suggested by the tester when the artist could not come up with one, and it was accepted by him. He, too, had volunteered in my class out of a desire to help out, and he, too, had no specific plan for the image. He blurred the image, brought out the trees in the lower left corner, then blackened the sky; he turned again to certain details such as dividing the swing at the bottom in two and moving the windows out of the houses, and finally ripped the landscape into pieces, leaving the black background, and added little pairs of eyes where the windows had been. Small-scale symbolism worked hand in hand with a broad-scale rendering of ominousness.

The son of a strict but fair university staff member, he lost his mother when he was three and gained a stepmother who, to us, resembles the nightmarish ones from Grimms' fairy tales. She was highstrung, critical, aggressive, and punishing, sticking his face into his bed if he would wet it; the child would hide in his room for long periods of time. The father may have tried to protect him (he is unsure), but he, too, was aggressive in his way and punished the boy with a belt. Matters were exacerbated by a racial conflict: the stepmother was white, the original family black—the old terms bring us closer to the image—and her relatives were overtly and aggressively racist. Father and stepmother are now divorced, and the son has controlled his anger and is now planning a professional career.

The image is dotted with individual reminders of his childhood— the broken swing, the eyes peering out of lonely, dark rooms—and informed by a divided, dark view of life. He has dreams in which there is something missing, and finds himself wishing he had known his mother better before she died. Suppressing his anger—he knows that he suppresses it, because in films he likes violence a lot—has been achieved at a cost: he is sometimes quite depressed. And the mix of all these burdens seems best expressed in this rambling, albeit powerful, image.

A raw and violent picture by Goya entitled *Saturn Devouring His Children* is behind another transformation of the Village scene. The young man—an art student—was aware only of the wish to keep his work realistic, so he thought first of changing the color of the sky— fuschia at first, dark blue later. Only when the sky was dark blue did he notice that the castle reminded him of the recent film *Kafka*, and he conceived of the monster figure on which he spent most of his time. He also drew a fire on the parapet, a face on the wall, a tiny figure above it, and finally little pink dots connecting the figures. The big creature was always a Goya creature to him, and when asked to explain, he reminded us of *Saturn Devouring his Son* [sic]. The title **Goya** seems natural.

Although his symbolism is quite specific, he cannot explain it further. He is aware that the monster is coming from the castle to the village below, but what he may do to it, or what the other elements may represent, remains unclear; the face on the wall is perhaps from *Apocalypse Now*. The son of much older parents, he identifies with his father's "very aggressive" ways of gathering information although he is very distant from him in age and tastes. He describes his mother in objective terms such as "positive" and "optimistic". The interviewer has to work hard to elicit information, and we are left with only hints about the meaning of the work: we find it in his sense that as an adolescent he had to break away forcefully, especially from his father; in his doubt that humanity can pull itself out from destroying the world; in his sense that in relationships one will die unless one makes oneself happy—and, above all, in his avoidance of aggression in real life while searching for violence in films.

Perhaps the monster is some sort of punishment for his rebellion; we can only suggest it, and cannot know for certain. But the dark tone, the vagueness of formulation and reluctance to know oneself, as well as the undertone of suppressed aggression, link him closely to the participants we have looked at so far.

The Sicily Pictures

If a castle towering over small buildings suggests the family as seen by the child, an open desert landscape invites filling it with projections. With open space, there are few constraints on where the projections might be placed, which in itself may invite an episodic appearance, but as we have seen, an unplanned process can be revealed in different ways.

In *Smudgie-Pie*—an evocative title redolent as much of gustatory pleasure as of confusion—the unplanned process is revealed predictably, in the disconnected superimposition of figures on various parts of the landscape. This was not done by plan, but by a response to a chance event, a visit to the Monterey aquarium; that is why there are so many fish, and why the young woman, also an art student, has been doing "fish and stuff" lately in her work. She is quite frustrated throughout the time that she works—something that seems out of proportion to her skill in representation—and just goes around the picture, as she says, trying to fill in various areas. When she has done so, and when in response to some request for help the experimenter accidentally zooms in for her on a blank portion of the sky, she says, "save that: that's my picture"; the blowup is so fluid and empty that she calls it "smudgie-pie". We did save it, but it is less informative than the picture that just preceded it, and so we reproduce that one.

She lives in a confusing family and has a hard time describing it. It does consist of her mother, stepfather, and siblings by two other men; the second stepfather is so recent that she barely knows him, but she does know the first stepfather well, and can describe him only too vividly. She has been good friends with her real father (whose "little daughter" she has always been), who left the family when she was two, but dislikes the stepfather, who is cold, intellectual, religious—and was outrageously dishonest in the way he appropriated her mother's property before they divorced. (She had to testify in court that she had found evidence of his attempts to destroy an agreement by which the parents shared the income from their joint work.) All the family members have pulled away because he is—she says this with her first display of emotion—an evil man. For years her mother used to tell her that she could not go to college and it was only a last-minute gift from her grandparents that enabled her to do so. Now that the mother is again remarried, she remains concerned with money and turns increasingly to alcohol, and this makes communication with her difficult; but she will not allow our artist to have contact with the first stepfather either.

The losses in her life have been less dramatic than cumulative, it would seem. Having lost both fathers and not gained the third, and being left with an unreliable mother, she has every reason to be confused and emotionally distant. She has reason to be angry, too, which she is in ample measure ("I just get pissed, I just get pissed, and want to tell people off!"), and she handles it by having a beer, or drawing something, or listening to loud music.

Lightning seems like a more focused title, but the lines which represent the flashes come late in the image making process, after the painter's original intention had been satisfied: to make the whole image darker. He works by "pouring" dark colors into areas, smudging, then darkening some more, and almost always by using filters. The sinuous lines coming from the upper left are discovered late, and he comments that they represent an explosion coming from the lightning, but the emphasis remains on the darkness.

His later interview is the briefest and least informative one we have seen. We do learn that his parents are both accountants, that the father used to be stern and never talked much, and that the mother is more outgoing; he can at least talk with her about his feelings. He reveals in an off-hand manner that he was cared for by his grandparents until he was about twelve.

He opens up to us only when discussing his two closest friends, who share his most important interests: animation, comics, movies, and guns. They had known each other since first grade, since, that is, they had started playing Dungeons and Dragons together, and now they play futuristic science fiction games, in particular a "dark feature" game in which they take specific roles and write scenarios for themselves that go on and on for years; they imagine a worst-case economic scenario for the world and follow their characters through years of development.

There seems to be an adolescent quality to his thinking and imagining, and it does seem connected with the handling of aggression. When we ask him about a recent example of how he handles anger, he says that he got mad not long ago and just drew a couple of pictures to burn it off: a couple of knights, of whom one had a sword and was poised for battle; and yes, that one represented him. He is otherwise unaggressive—but then again he likes monster films and "dark feature" films such as *Terminator 2*. We find him consistent with this group, but he gives us little to go on to understand him as an individual.

The woman who made the picture she calls **Growing** is, on the contrary, open to us and thoughtful and insightful. To make her image she borrows freely and loosely from the Leaves picture, neither connecting the borrowings with each other nor integrating them with the Sicily landscape. Admittedly she had an initial focus—the persimmon she calls a peach—and was going to "nestle it into a little group of leaves that we lost somewhere" but soon wanders off: ... "I knew I had other things to do. Things to do and places to go within the image. I knew I was going somewhere." In this she is typical of this cluster, but in one respect she is uniquely herself: all the parts she incorporates into her image—all the parts she comments on in any of the images she looks at first—are sexual. In the present picture a little black triangle looks like a woman's crotch; there is a breast here, a butt there, a baby elsewhere.

Disowned as she reached maturity by a domineering and violent father who was as controlling as he appeared generous, she has not spoken to him for years. She believes that he beat her the most because he was sexually attracted to her; and he certainly manipulated her by stratagems such as promising to give her what she wanted as long as she behaved, and then not giving it to her because she behaved well only to get it. She lost all trust in him through such episodes, yet her mother failed her in her way, too. Beautiful, talented, aesthetic, and probably fragile, she gave up fighting her father, took ill, and died quite young (under circumstances our painter considers suspicious).

Even if we wish to allow for some dramatization, we have to recognize the experience of pain, cruelty, and disillusionment, and even if we wish to take note of her sexual projections, we can see them as not unexpectable defenses against a manipulated childhood. Like the other participants from this cluster, she is loose in her image construction and she does respond to considerable pain; unlike them, she is not preoccupied with something else such as anger, but rather is loose in her free associative thinking. Her anger is there, too, and it is easily felt and expressed, but it seems a less important part of her makeup.

The Leaves Pictures

The original Leaves picture seemed likely to challenge the participants to a formal treatment emphasizing rhythmic repetition, or to invite an episodic treatment, but our volunteers seem to have responded to the invitation, not to the formal challenge: both pictures[1] are episodic, even incoherent.

Monogram (Fig. 28 below) is a title that occurred to us after the young woman who made it said that she would have cut off the triangular part in the upper right of the picture had she had the time—the corner, she said, was not finished and therefore not part of the picture. We could see no difference between the part and the whole for a long time, but finally noticed that the part was unmarked by any identifying transformations; it was, as it were, not yet monogrammed. Such a treatment is episodic in the extreme, and we found when we interviewed her later not only a specific emphasis in the family on monogramming all the objects in the house, but also an identity which had been incompletely patched together from roles she had been asked to play from her childhood on. This literal and metaphorical unconnectedness is perhaps a special form of episodic treatment and it seems to deserve a closer look; her detailed, even voluminous responses to our interview make it possible, and we shall look at her again a little later.

Tears, too—the artists' own title—is episodic, but with a poignant, lacrymose, even violent cast. Not sure at first what she wanted to do, the young woman got an idea from the bottom right corner but did not tell us what it was. She first strengthened the outlines in the whole picture with filters and then began drawing drops dripping off one of the leaves; she then began to outline a nearby leaf in red, saying that she was putting makeup on it like Tammy Fae Baker. Soon the makeup was joined by finely drawn teeth, and next to the now complete mouth she drew a pair of eyes—"a face of bewilderment". Other drops from other leaves followed. She was now ready to tell us what was going on: "I'm trying to get the person to be the president; some people will agree, some will be amazed, and some will end up crying." She went on to develop the fantasy and to duplicate the mouth twice more, each time blurred. Working on another leaf in green, she said that it looked like a taco, and that she was hungry. Having finished, she explained that her whole week has been one where "one person is telling everyone else what they should do", and that the teardrops signified one person imposing his beliefs on another.

---

[1] There were in fact three episodic images based on this picture, but a substantial loss of the data on one of the participants precludes any meaningful presentation; there were also two episodic Temple pictures, as we shall see, but the data are complete on one of them only.

Her family's turbulence, and her painful history, help us understand the anger and the resistance. The adopted daughter of middle class parents, she easily volunteers two early memories which come back repeatedly in her dreams: in one she is waiting in line in an orphanage in Viet Nam, waiting to go to the bathroom, and in the other she is walking around a building in the orphanage and sees a general shooting a man in the head and back several times. To this trauma was added a history of angry conflicts with her adoptive mother—conflicts to which she knows she contributed. When they first met, she pulled the mother's hair and spat in her face; in the long run her mother, however, came to control her relentlessly throughout her childhood. She deprived her of food if she did not exercise enough for her ballet classes, sent her away for the summer to lose weight only to find that her daughter rebelled and ate voraciously, and all in all made her weight an issue that led to screaming fights. The parents argued with each other as well, and we are not surprised to hear her say, "that was our family—a battlefield."

It must be noted that she speaks of these painful matters with insight and a sense that she is coping. But the dynamics with which she is struggling are nevertheless dominated by unexpurgated anger—stronger certainly than that of the other participants—a gnawing hunger, and no reassurance of stability through a coherent family. Her picture is angry and sad, and it is unable to draw upon a sense of the world's coherence.

The Garden Pictures

An ambiguous image, "Garden" may seem either a promise of earthly delights or a threat of dark dangers, depending on whether one responds to the profuse flora or the black spaces in between, and we need not be surprised if some artists react to both.

So it is with **Garden of Chanterelle** (Fig. 29, below), an apparently happy fairy tale made murky by a pair of eyes peering out of the darkness. The young woman who created it knew that she was putting herself in the center of it: the hair of the fairy with the diaphanous wings is red, like hers. She stands on a blade of grass surrounded by bright plants and cute animals—and yet a fire licks at her from the bottom ("but it won't hurt her") and a wolf peers at her waiting to gobble her up.

She had written the word "kill" on the picture and then erased it, and she refers to her mother as a "killer" mom. All is not happy in the picture, then, nor seems to be in the family, and as we shall see there is a good bit of barely contained anger in her life. We shall also see that both she and the family have responded to a drastic loss in income they had suffered when she was eight. She is a person who expresses herself volubly and yet precisely, so she seems very much worth presenting in detail. For now, it seems important to establish the presence of anger and loss in the pollyannish, regressive defense.

A much calmer atmosphere prevails in a picture called **Reflections**, which was abstracted from the same photograph. It was painted by a woman who, like the maker of *Growing*, was in her early forties, but its indefinite character resulted from the frustration of a plan rather than a free-associative meandering. The original plan was to get rid of the darkness that she feared and to create a path down which she could walk, but she had difficulty doing that convincingly and abandoned the project altogether; trying out one filter after another, she then became attracted by the possibility of diffusing the image, did so, selected a portion that gave her a good composition, and was done. Her title refers both to the reflections she intended to draw and to her mood—she had considered "Pensive" instead. She worked carefully and on a small scale, seemed unwilling to experiment, and thought that we could have been more helpful with the image making process.

The only child in her family, she grew up very close to her father— "his little girl"—who was a quiet, generous, hard-working man who worked seven days a week and provided for his family, but was not very demonstrative. She has always tried to be like him, that is, conscientious, quiet, intent on thinking things through (in her words, perhaps too much so). She volunteers that she never felt unloved or unwanted, but that her mother had always worried that she might feel abandoned; this is not explained further, but suggests that the child was alone a good bit. Her mother was young-thinking and open-minded, but also overprotective, and the young child grew up dependent and worrying that if she did something wrong, her mother would die. No one in the family ever argued; "you either ignored it or denied it". The parents did not need to discipline her because she was her own disciplinarian—she even set her own curfews as an adolescent.

We can see ample reasons for her cautious approach to the image: the family's anxious protectiveness probably evoked as much anxiety as it controlled, and our artist grew up seeking peace and quiet. She says that she sought it here, in this image, and we learn that she has more reasons than usual for seeking it now: her father had died a few months before. One of her present goals is to become more relaxed.

She is not quite like the other members of her group, then; she is not responding to an early loss or a seething anger. If her image is unfocused, it is because she has defocused it; hard and potentially disturbing forms have been made soft and gentle. Rather than being episodic, the image is made diffuse and reassuring.

We return, however, to a relentlessly episodic treatment in a picture that is based on our training photograph: a temple ruin we simply called Temple. Although our volunteers were encouraged to choose from pictures they had not yet worked on, some insisted on returning to what they had already gotten to know; among these is the painter of the next image.

A Temple Picture

Transforming a temple picture into a **Monster** may not seem straightforward. The result was certainly not intended, the painter being attracted by the ruin itself and deciding to work by simply "sticking colors or shapes in places where I thought I would like them and then hoping it would come together later." Some of her work was done under extreme magnification, some by repeated pastings. Eventually she had put it so many colors that it began to look more like her own image than the original one, and she began to visualize what was going to happen. When she was little, she recollects, her mother's friends—psychologists like her—would play scribbles with her to keep her busy and would find animals and shapes in them, and so she finds the monster in the rectangle below the six green boomerangs in the place where the triglyph had been. She also draws fish in some of the blue patches and they "still appear to be swimming, not being eaten." Asked if the image connects with her life in any way, she says, "I suppose it is a bit chaotic looking in total. My life is feeling really chaotic right now."

There is something counterphobic about her off-hand remarks that we would wish to understand better. Certainly a fear of being eaten, if it is there, would be quite inaccessible to us, but the fear of a monster might be closer to the surface. She does tell us that when she was little she used to be frightened of her father, who presented himself as a demanding authority figure and had a bad temper to match, and perhaps that is a sufficient explanation. But we are here more interested in what makes her work episodic. There is a mention of anger, which she handles either by doing something self-destructive such as cutting her nails very short or throwing away things she is fond of, or by turning to collage (yes, as here); and there is an early loss, a move from the city where she was born to where she lives now, which she describes as traumatic.

Still, we do not wish to stretch the parallels. A psycho-biological explanation offers itself as well: she has been diagnosed as dyslexic and dysgraphic. It is just possible that she might find it difficult to construct a coherent image even if she wanted to, and that her mother's friends' habit of encouraging her to find forms in scribbles was a tacit or explicit recognition of this disability. Our inclination is to see the explanations as complementary: the fantasies are, after all, of a monster and of fish that might be eaten. And her life *is* feeling chaotic.

THE PSYCHOLOGICAL DYNAMICS OF THIS CLUSTER

Of the two qualities of image making that we wished to explain in this cluster—the negative mood and the disconnected form—the mood is the easier to explain. It seems connected in all but the last two subjects with an early pain, loss or deprivation. This was the earliest and deepest substratum of our artists' makeup, and it was followed—now in all but one individual—by a childhood spent with a cold, or distant, or demanding and sometimes even frightening, father. The dark mood was joined by *an inhibited, distant or dainty, mode of working—a mode that reflected an anger that either seethed or was being contained.*

To understand the episodic organization we must look at these same lives from another vantage point. Our painters seem to relate to others in a tenuous way—here living with conspicuous denial, there living with unreliability, elsewhere with clinging fathers. If we look at their relations with peers, something we have not made part of our narrative so far, almost none of our participants are both attached and sexual. Some are of course altogether unattached, while others are not yet sexual although they have boyfriends or girlfriends, and still others separate sex from attachment and either have one partner for sex and another for closeness, or make sex the focus of the one relationship they do have; for them, sex is a mere release of tension. The exceptions are the two older women (the painters of *Growing* and *Reflections*), one of whom sexualizes most of her experiences and the other of whom is only now losing her fear of sex.

We are brought back to the formulation in our introductory chapter: *the disconnected form of their images seems, then, to be a symbol of the incoherence of their connections with others.*

To make this generalization we have had to abstract from the reality of our participants' lives and to ignore some of the fine variants, indeed the human flavor, of their way of being. We are now ready to look closely at the form of two images and the lives of which they are part.

MONOGRAM

I have already said that the young woman who created this image—I shall call her Deborah—proceeded in an altogether episodic manner: one kind of transformation here, another there, with no apparent wish to connect them nor any sense of their not fitting together. Some leaves were outlined, others had their texture transformed by filters, the persimmon was turned into a mosaic, a form in the shape of a "c" was drawn next to it (seen next to the blue dot it became an ear and the white shape became a gorilla's head), a drawn leaf was labeled "leaf" for clarity—and a little airplane was drawn coming in from bottom right. Her comments while working confirm our impression that the work was to be assembled without plan: "I like Leaves because each has its own identity, and I can do something different with each ... . I have a hard time making one piece with one scene—that's why I like several things going on." And she made clear, too, that she likes bright colors, and that she wished her image to be happy. A hint of rebellion against constraints was offered in her comment on the child-like quality of some of her favorite areas: "the strokes that look like something a child would do with a crayon, ... not so regimented or regulated— little children don't have to stay within the lines."

In the discussion that followed immediately afterward Deborah confirmed her preference for independent parts, whose advantage is that she can make them look the way she wants them to look, and volunteered that the artwork she does from time to time is designed to make her happy—she just likes to draw colorful little happy images. But she does pause over the triangle in the upper right, which to her is troublesome and should have been cut off; she cannot say why, except that there was nothing in it that she could like.

Later, when we discussed the process in our staff meeting, we puzzled over the triangle, because it was the one thing we could not understand. It did seem to us to have less evidence of personal presence, and since the image did not have a title (nor did it have to, except for ease of reference), I suggested "Monogram". Later this proved to have more meaning than we had thought. In the psychodynamic interview Deborah mentioned—unasked—that in her house most objects were monogrammed; it seemed to us that this served to establish possession. Now her transformations of the objects in her image seemed like so many monogramming acts, and the upper right area seemed unsatisfactory because it was unpossessed still.

This is of course only one meaning of her episodic approach; others became clear as she told us about her life. Both her parents are

Figure 28. Monogram

professionals, busy and well to do; her father is a powerful man who is always in control. Having said that, she says that he is not *controlling*, which would suggest enjoying controlling other people, but simply and naturally in control. She would not describe him as affectionate either, although she adds that he understands what kids growing up need; she recalls that neither of his parents had been affectionate themselves and that this made it hard for him to relate to his daughter as a girl. She resembles him in this sense of dominance: she does not want power, but notices that things run smoother in groups when she is in charge. The two clash often, given their similar personalities, but after much arguing she usually backs down—in order to validate him. He makes clear that he does not like shouting and when things get out of hand, he simply says, "enough, we're having a good time", and our young artist begins to feel like a mother to him, having to pat and nurture him. We shall understand this reversal of roles presently.

Her mother is described as very strong but also as a loner, an excellent business person, very protective of her children and very close to Deborah. She *seems* harsh and aggressive because she likes to deal with issues concretely and immediately and leave emotions for later; Deborah finds it easier to say that she seems that way to others, but reveals some of her own feelings about her as well.

Describing her childhood she says, "as a child, I had very little connection with my parents; we did a lot of traveling together, ... but I was never treated as a child; I never had the chance to be a child ... . I knew they loved me but I never felt love from them, as a child, just because there was no affection going on ... . I was feeling shunned by my father because he was always away." As she grew older, the sense of being deprived of her childhood became even stronger because she was assigned responsibility for her siblings, having to discipline them and write all the school notes for them—and yet in another way she was not allowed to develop a sense of competence: she could not go past the driveway, cross streets, or go to school by herself, or even wash her own hair or cook meals. As she puts it, "their form of discipline was to keep me helpless."

To try to get them to pay attention to her, "because I wanted to make them proud of me", she developed very high goals. And to bridge the distance between her and her father, she would pick up his pastimes: whatever sport he did, and however often he changed it, she would become good at it herself.

Deborah has described all these painful matters without apparent feeling but with clear memory. She has helped us see that the happiness she has tried to impose on her image barely masks her expectably depressive feelings, succeeding no better than monogramming its various parts. She has also enabled us to understand her episodic organization: deprived of a childhood and of the emotional closeness that it requires, she never quite came to know herself; chasing after her father—a moving target—she became many different things, none of which had any connection with her own self. Her identity was formed too early and of necessity was cobbled together from these isolated pieces, and the image she has made serves in some way as a portrait of herself. It is also a portrait of the way she understands her parents: although her description is informed by many acute observations, it also contains contradictions of which she is quite unaware. We would think that as her understanding becomes better integrated, greater wholeness—in image-making as well—will follow.

GARDEN OF CHANTERELLE

The work of "Eileen" seems more straightforwardly happy at first. She paints the checkerboard pattern on the ground, starts painting a flower purple, and remarks—revealing a loosely governing fantasy—that this is beginning to look like Alice in Wonderland stuff. She continues within that broad directive by working on various flowers and drawing the butterfly, and it must be said that she works with an aesthetic kind of discipline because she picks her colors only from the image itself, so as to remain within the range the image presents. About an hour after starting she decided to draw the fairy—a happy enough creature—with Eileen's red hair, green wings, and a magic wand, but also poised precipitously on the blade of grass. She then colors a lot of leaves with different colors, and having discovered the Find Edges filter, goes on a "spree" of finding edges. The "sinister" eyes soon follow (and she catches herself getting angry), as do the mushroom and the fire ("which won't hurt the fairy"). Trying out the lettering option, she writes the word "Kill", then erases it.

Having finished, she tells us about the experience. She liked the Leaves picture as a starting point because "it had a lot of black for a great background". She likes the objects she has created: the butterfly, the mushroom, the road, the eyes, the snail—but does not mention the image as a whole. She thinks that she had started without a plan, but does remember that she likes fairies, and that the past weekend she and a friend pretended that they were fairies and elves; the mushroom is connected with her grandmother, who always had mushroom magnets, and the eyes do seem to be watching her. But

Figure 29. Garden of Chanterelle

her general approach is, she says, to just "like objects or colors or chaos", and here she just "filled in the spaces with whatever popped up in her brain".

Eileen's father is a pretty tall man with a bad temper, who is really good with little kids and animals but also dominating, and therefore not good with teenagers. Like him, she loves kids and animals, and like him she is stubborn, but she tries not to get as angry as he does. (She also had been "dad's little princess"—one of six in this cluster—and we mention this because we wonder if they had not been intimidated by their closeness to bad-tempered fathers.) Their relationship now is "respectful". It is much easier for her to describe her mother, however: she is "the coolest mom I know, ... her morals, her beliefs, and the way she loves her life are so pure ... she's also very accepting ... . She's also always believed in us no matter what our abilities—she's like a killer woman. She's focusing so much on helping our lives and stuff, instead of her own."

The adjective "killer" was used at the time as a general superlative, and one would not be inclined to read too much into it if it were not for the word "kill" which she had tried out on the surface of the picture. We do not doubt her admiration, nor do we insist that there must be more than a normal ambivalence there, but we do suspect an aggressive cast to her view of the world—the adjective, in any case, was not that common. We do learn that while the mother is saintly, Eileen is not (in her view); she is aggressive and strong, like her father. And we learn when we ask her about how she handles aggression that she needs to discharge it quite often, sometimes by dancing to hardcore music and, at present, having one boyfriend for friendship and another for sex. She recalls that one night she was "drunk and I was making out with this guy and I guess I was being really aggressive... and the next day [this guy] said, 'like, dude, if you wanted to, you could have totally raped me.' I was like, 'Oh my God ... .' "

Her aggressive feelings are, then, quite close to the surface. In what way can they help explain her episodic style? Our impression is that Eileen is strongly impulsive and the aggressive and loving feelings easily transform one into the other; the regressive, innocent fantasies seem like a good counterphobic defense against something angrier or more fearful, but there is darkness in the background and dangers lurk in it. Unlike the happier seeming reparations of the first cluster, the fantasies here alternate between the good and the bad, and she is confused. She does, by the way, "want children all the time", and her prominent fear is of being pushed; the life of her art is also the life of her everyday imagination.

EPILOGUE

Both Deborah and Eileen came in after we had brought the data together and asked about our interpretations. Deborah did so a few months after she had produced her image, while Eileen came in a year later. Deborah reacted to the equivalent of the interpretation we have made here with acceptance; she was perhaps surprised by its directness or incisiveness, but found nothing specifically new in it nor anything to object to. Eileen found that we had described her as she was at the time, but said that she had changed since then; she had been only a freshman, was still establishing a view of the world independent of her parents, and now feels more independent and mature. By this she means that she is less naïve and pollyannish; she can now admit that people can steal from her, that mean people can play mind games with her, and that her mother is not perfect. She can also be attracted to a guy both for friendship and for sex; and she is no longer compulsively attached to children. We wish we had asked her to do another image.

CHAPTER 5

Third Cluster

Bold, Flowing Process and the Direct Expression of Emotion

This cluster introduces image qualities we have not yet seen: bold execution and a flowing process. The images here are notable, that is, for their idiosyncratic handling and for the emotional response which they stimulate in the viewer (with these characteristics defining their boldness), and for the sense that their forms move diffusely within the frame (with these qualities, as well as with the unhesitating and fluid process by which the images had been constructed, defining their flowingness). It is as if the images had something to say—something immediate and direct, said without hesitation or perhaps with the certainty that it could be said.

A brief look at the images makes it clear why they would have been grouped together. In the six images based on the Village picture we see either a reign of destruction or dissolution (as in *The End of the World, Dragon Snow, My Rooftop, and Destitute Depot*) or a mood of despair (as in *Scream*), or—and this does seem different—a muted, somewhat joyless mood (*Scribbles*). In another two pictures, based on the Garden photograph (*Garden of Eve* and *Honeymoon*), we see a perfectly consistent, flowing and repetitive brushstroke which unifies the surface in a moving kind of swarm. In yet another two (*Chocolate Swirls* and *Whirlwinds*), we see unity achieved by a fuzzy, blurry kind of manipulation; in *Perceptions of an Inner World* we see less of a theme or story than a dense, airless space, but it, too is made mostly by blurring forms. In the final picture (*Split*), however, we have a floating, diaphanous, liquid abstraction. Only this picture does not seem fully to belong, and we see by reference to Table 5b in the appendix that the

Figure 30. The End of the World

Figure 31. Dragon Snow

Figure 32. My Rooftop

Figure 33. Destitute Depot

Figure 34. Scribbles

Figure 35. Garden of Eve

Figure 36. Chocolate Swirls

Figure 37. Whirlwinds

Figure 38. Perceptions of an Inner World

Figure 39. Split

image has some connection with cluster 7 as well; we shall look at the young man nevertheless.[1]

Apart from the last picture, then, the images here are connected by their consistent method. They are made "by hand", that is, by operations which resemble drawing, painting, or smudging. They have a kind of self-assurance that suggests practice and habit, and indeed when we look at the painters' academic interests we find that nine of the twelve are art majors. This of course raises a question we must address: could the method of working that we see here be more a product of artistic experience than psychodynamics, or of both in some equal measure? A comparison with cluster 6, where all the members are art majors, will be crucial in this respect, and we shall see that their way of doing art, and their psychodynamics as well, will be different; and of course with the three individuals here who are not art majors we cannot invoke their artistic habits at all. So whatever role an adopted style may play in this cluster, certain shared dynamics will propel it, and it is these that we shall now look at.

---

[1] Two artists who were assigned to this cluster have been excluded from this analysis, because they could just as well have been assigned to other clusters. Another partici- pant has had to be omitted from this discussion because he left the university before we could do his psychodynamic interview. This is a pity, because he exemplified in the clearest possible way some of characteristics we see in the others; his emotions were so accessible that he fell in love with his experimenter on the spot and proceeded to do a picture of her, hoping both that she would recognize it and fail to. And yes, he, too, was an art student working with a loose but steady and consistent hand stroke.

We shall find that, with two exceptions, the members of this cluster have few controls over the expression of their emotions; they either see themselves as emotionally expressive in general, or tell us that they are driven specifically by anger—and that they have a parental model for this. The availability of emotion, particularly anger, seems to be their driving force, while the habit of working with consistent strokes of the hand gives that emotion a direct expression.

THE PSYCHOLOGICAL PROCESS SEEN INDIVIDUALLY

Thus, the young woman who produced *The End of the World* is the daughter of two quite different parents: a controlling father, and an emotionally open, impulsive mother. Beginning her image work with wisps of air blurring the top of the roofs of the castle, she started to see the air as smoke, and having gone this far decided that the smoke might just indicate fire (but she then pulled back from saying that it actually did). With this fantasy firmly in place, she could then simultaneously shore up the rock on which the castle sits and break a part of it away so that it fell into the abyss; then, with this much destruction accomplished, she could plant barely visible little flowers in the rock fissures to civilize the destruction. With the world crumbling, she said, the flowers were there to take over again.

It is the mother that she is close to and loves without reservation. Her first words describing her mother are "She's great, I love her … she's great, she's my best friend … she's an artist, working at home, so she was always there." She likes her mother's zest for life: "She likes to have fun and just, you know, lets you know you're living so you might as well have fun at it." Warming up to her subject, she adds, "She can be crazier than me and I really admire that about her. I wouldn't mind being just like her." The father is an exacting and controlling science teacher who likes to argue, so the two women—there are no other children— ignore him when he does. Our impression is that they collude in this way quite cheerfully; they just have different ways of doing things than he. In any case, the mother and father have a good relationship, admittedly fighting a lot but also being "each other's true loves."

When asked whether she is emotionally expressive, the young woman says that she is not good at hiding what she is feeling, but adds that when she was little everyone always said that she was moody. It is the expression of anger, however, that is striking. Rather than merely telling us that she is easily irritated, she demonstrates: she bursts out and yells, "stop it! You're bugging me!" To describe her disappointment with her first boyfriend, she shouts, "you can't trust anybody!" We have the impression that she accepts her anger quite cheerfully, and that she balances it with a good capacity for love (for her mother and boyfriend, for example). She can feel strong love and anger at the same time, as when she says, "I have a lot of friends I really hate." It is that expressiveness, as well as that balance between love and anger, that inform the balance of destruction and regrowth we see in her image.

An equally accepting demonstration of rampage controlled by humor is seen in **Dragon Snow**. Not a planned picture, it was at least directed by the need to reduce some of the happiness in it; the artist stained the sky purple and worked on darkening the landscape and making two houses in the center stand out by their pastel colors. She began to draw the dragon and then people leaning out of their windows waving their arms. Then she did something quite by accident: she managed to "pour" white paint into a part of the image. Startled at first, she then decided to accept it as white snow, and went on to integrate the snow into her fantasy. She drew a few more little people and they were now waving because their houses were burning. Yet it all ends on a cheerful note of denial: the dragon is only using spray paint ("being creative") and the people would almost rather their houses simply burnt down than being painted by a dragon-artist; and a skier whizzes by, unconcerned.

Her parents seem the mirror images of the previous ones. Her mother is the rule maker and disciplinarian, an obsessive woman who is always cleaning the house; our artist calls her "anal retentive". Nor is she open about her emotions. Her father, on the other hand, although competitive in his business, is easy-going at home and even childish; he was the one to take his daughter to see Muppet movies, and he is the one she got her artistic side from. He also seems to be the source of the image of the partner she would like to have—someone goofy, unafraid to look stupid in public, sensitive to her mood shifts.

Unlike the painter of *End of the World*, however, this young woman is not generally expressive of emotion. What she does have close to the surface is anger. These days she lets her anger fester, but she used to yell in order to express it. Now she like violent films such as the Terminator series; when asked what films she considers romantic, she gives examples of what anyone else would consider violent as well—films with the actor Van Damme. Speaking of her reaction to surprises, she remembers being surprised at her eighteenth birthday party by a stripper. "I guess I could have been calm and cool … [after the guy interrupted the TV watching and stripped], I must have been five minutes on the ground threatening to kill everyone in the place ... but in between I was enjoying it." And yes, she does identify with the dragon in her picture.

My Rooftop is a much sadder picture, created by scribbling, smudging, greying down, and drawing—the drawing being confined to the swing, the bridge, and the little person on the roof. The picture has a mood that its painter, a young woman, likes: grey, dreary and rainy— and yet in some sense safe; safe and scary at the same time, she adds. She had chosen the Village picture to work with because the other pictures were either too open, so they didn't feel safe, or too closed, so that she could not even enter. Talking quite spontaneously about the image, she adds, "I think that figure up there is me, it just sort of feels alone to me, like sitting on my own roof away from everything else ... . At first I just wanted to be over there alone, like I didn't want to have anything to do with these other houses, and then I drew this bridge and I couldn't decide: was it my way to get over there, or for other people and other things to get to me? ... It totally reminds me of the house I grew up in and it's right behind me and feels really haunted to me."

No interpretation could improve on the one this student proposed, and it is testimony to the availability of her feelings—at least certain feelings—that she can so clearly tie the picture to her past. All her art is this personal, she says, whether it is this evocative or not: "I realize that when I do art it is really personal; it is usually about me and how I feel." Her life story is equally transparent. The youngest of four children, she lost her mother when she was a baby and was raised by her father. She realizes that this must have been difficult for him, but knows also that he did not discharge his obligation very well: never able to say what he expected of his daughters, he would wait till they did something he did not like and then he would "freak out on us and yell and get really angry ... emotionally he was very abusive and out of control, and I think his drinking added to that." Now he is content to be discontent, lonely and depressed—and very angry.

When asked about her emotional expressiveness, she responds only in terms of anger: "When I was really young, I used to be really expressive, to the point of screaming and throwing things and having temper tantrums. But at some point it wasn't OK to be that way, and ... I held everything in. And now I feel like I am getting back to that place of being a four-year-old and being really emotionally out with how I feel."

That she should be driven by anger, most of which is directed at her father, needs no further explanation. It bears adding, however, that her childhood feelings were locked in place, as it were; no one in her family seems to have helped her assimilate her feelings of sadness and grief—which she says are so intense that they get in the way of her relationships—the father not allowing her to be sad and no one, not even her sisters, ever talking about the mother's death. We believe that she was spared a more unhappy adulthood by a loving, kind grandmother who put all the love she had felt for her daughter into her four grandchildren. Her art might have been more reparative, like that of the participants in cluster 1, if she had wanted to substitute a made-up reality for the remembered one, but of this she seems incapable.

With **Scream** (Fig. 40), a picture that combines the bound-up stasis of the figure on the right with the emotional outburst of the one on the left, we are again in a world where all emotion, not specifically or principally anger, is being expressed. The young man who created it is very sensitive to others' pain, and indeed he had come in that morning upset over the news from Sarajevo; it colored his whole, long and rambling, work with us. He had been like that ever since he can remember, crying, for example, when his mother would cry. The rawness of his feelings is mirrored in the transparency of his image, and no feats of interpretation are required to see the connection. Since, however, his memories are as accessible as his feelings, and his ability to put them into words is equally well developed, we shall return to him in greater detail at the end of the chapter.

Anger again, not emotion in general, is the feeling accessible to the young man who transformed the Burgundy village into a **Destitute Depot**. His way of working involved constant motion and blurring, and his attention was directed at first to the windows, which he either blackened or moved here and there, and to the sky, which he made orange to indicate either sunrise or sunset. He began to smudge the edges of the roofs to indicate that they were evaporating—and with an interplay of raw emotion and defense reminiscent of the painter of *The End of the World*, he denied that they were burning. He also painted a house rising above the landscape on the right, two pinnacles on the left, and wisps of smoke connecting everything. When he was done, he said, vaguely but with a sense of relevance to his life at present, that "it looks like stopped time, ... as opposed to a still life, things disappearing, roaring apart or forming a model of change—the future is the building that's hovering ... . Some windows are still in flotation, forming, no roots." He explained that he was himself in the process of changing, working very hard at his painting unlike before, and that this represents a drastically different life pattern for him, a complete reorganization. In effect, the building rising on the right is himself, moving upward but without moorings.

But the picture represents the future no more than the past: his father is described as distant, weird, and eccentric when the young man was a child, and now into a mid-life crisis complete with drugs; for the young man he has essentially gone off the deep end. His mother is conservative, religious, even more introverted than the father, but he had at least lived with her after the parents' divorce and is quite close to her now. All in all he identifies more with her than with him, although he has left the church to which both parents and all his sisters still faithfully adhere. Having dropped out of school, he is back now. He sees himself as easily annoyed, wanting to "scream for three hours" during a student critique of art work, normally doing a lot of swearing to express anger—always enjoying being pissed or irritated. His favorite movies are "splatter" movies, grizzly, disgusting, gory, bloody, violent movies.

Art had not been his major until he discovered that he was better at it than at biology, and in this he differs from the other artists represented here. It has helped him find himself and it is expected to be his career. One may presume that for a while it will remain somewhat raw and angry; his only regret about his image is that he did not "set the building on fire".

The young woman who painted **Scribbles** over the Village landscape began in a painterly manner, with the "brush", and in fact did not want to learn about any of the other tools; she simply worked with a particular stroke or gesture throughout the session. She had chosen the picture for its muted range of tones, and as she worked she chose her colors purely from this original range, with some black and white added. The final product has vigor in the two flows of brushstrokes outward from the center—or possibly inward—but also a somewhat bleak sky and a lemon/grey sun. This image, and the process by which it was done, do seem different; they seem less informed by emotion and more by a steady habit of working.

They are, indeed, different; the young woman describes a family that pushes achievement, and reveals a personal style in her speech that is steady, rambling, and somewhat unrelenting. Her father is a workaholic, highly focused and even obsessive; but he is also supportive of all that she wants to do, and this includes art. She recalls having always drawn as a child—on placemats in restaurants, for example—and makes a connection with the bedtime stories he would tell her. Her mother is obsessive, too, she says, but more in the sense of being devoted to her children's development; she made sure the homework was done, had the children enroll in various classes and try various activities and musical instruments to see what they would like, and encouraged them not to quit; "we were always on schedules, all the time". Our painter, too, is a little obsessive like her parents, and can see the connection in her art.

She returns to her image as she describes her father's obsessiveness. "It's like in the painting that I did: I was just getting into it and I just wanted to keep going; but then, I don't know, like maybe not, whatever." This first expression of uncertainty, or first denial of something she had just thought, turns out to mark her way of describing her life to us. She is long and rambling, complete and detailed, yet sometimes uncertain; she seems unable to stop. It would be difficult to see her as driven by emotion or memory, and easier to see her as driven by tension: describing the way she talks to her family on the phone, she says, "we're all just kind of tense, you know, like we easily start getting into arguments." That style seems to explain more about her image than does the felt experience of pain or anger. It should be said, however, that when given the opportunity to add anything she wanted to the interview that had not been adequately dealt with, she chose to mention anger: she thought it was a more important emotion than she had said at first, and that she felt it more than she realized.

The students who had chosen to work with the Village picture seemed to see a suggestion of their family, or of their present relation to their family, in its opposition between the high and mighty castle and the low houses beneath it. Four of them were very close to their family while the fifth (*Destitute Depot*) was trying to rip himself out of the embrace of its legacy; the sixth, likewise close, seemed to portray the family style more than its emotional charge. To this suggestion of family they all responded with a self-assured mode of working, and produced images that satisfy the viewer by their consistency—and yet also disturb by their anger, expressed sometimes gently, sometimes humorously, at other times drastically.

The next group of two, who worked on the Garden picture, is even more consistent in its style: in each case the images are built up from short, wiggly strokes. The two pictures are happy on the surface, but in fact reveal a balance between playfulness and anger.

Our oldest participant was a woman in her early forties who has returned to the university after raising a child and was eager for new experiences and perspectives. It is the question of perspective that animates her image, *The Garden of Eve*. Unsure at first of her goals—in part because she normally works from the model—she was nevertheless struck by the mystery of the ground level view of the garden, and began to wonder what might be in the background. What she discovered, by drawing, were two beasts in the back—not terribly nasty ones—and an intrusive, colossal foot in the front. She worked fast, with a self-assured handling of the stylus, and for stylistic consistency made sure that the colors she worked with came from the picture itself.

She is the daughter of what seems to be an exceptional couple: people now in their sixties who are so close they are "still honeymooning"; they had met and married young, always agreed on everything, and only recently have they begun to do things apart. She identifies more with her father, a very playful man who, at least when he was home, was very attentive to his family, and who, even now, is "still like a three-year-old; he is very bad in restaurants, he plays with the silverware, threatens food fights … ." Her mother was the disciplinarian—"the one who would yell at us"—never playful, more like a partner than a mother; now she no longer works and has the time to be a tennis bum. Our artist certainly appreciates her father's playfulness and identifies with it, and we hope not to intrude into the playfulness of her art work unduly by noting that many of her other memories are also about anger: fighting like cats and dogs with her brother ("my beloved brother, whom I wanted to kill"), her mother blowing a fuse and storming out of the room for fifteen minutes, her own physical aggressiveness as a girl, and her present tendency to explode verbally when angry. She had seen her mother cry only a few times, but "anger was something that I saw expressed very well."

She has "always drawn or painted" and intends to continue. She may not be very expressive of her emotions, but she feels them deeply, if unclearly: "I think that very often my emotions confuse me, so I don't know if I am happy or sad or angry or whatever … . I feel what I feel and then I look at it in an interior way." In the present picture, she seemed open to the possibility that the world will surprise her: "I guess the meaning is … that here you are kind of walking along in life, in your own world, admiring what you are admiring, and there is this whole other world going on that may or may not have anything to do with you."

A parents' honeymoon is also mentioned by the young woman who painted a chair next to a table—with both objects nearly obscuring the original view of the garden—the whole vigorous and cheerful and bucolic but for the electrical outlet at the right. She explained that the outlet was there for realism, and that the chair was one that the parents had bought for each other on their honeymoon; the subject matter and title of the image then become **Honeymoon** (Fig. 41). Her father, we shall see, is also very playful and her mother practical and serious, and she, too, has a "lot of anger inside her." We shall look at her life, the interplay between playfulness and emotion, and the purposes of her art, in greater detail later.

Three images were the product of blurring. The young man who swirled up the black and brown concoction he came to call **Chocolate Swirls** in fact started with the Sicily landscape. His choice of Sicily seemed fortuitous—Italy had been on his mind lately, with his study of the Aeneas myth and his girl friend being in Italy—but he called it fate. He did not know what to do with it other than to blur it, and this he did both by hand and by using blurring filters; the process was both playful and destructive, and as he said later, the process was everything. He remarked that he wanted to break things up and make them unrecognizable, and noted that smudging, in this sense, is like playing God. He reflected some of his art training, or rather his acceptance of it, by insisting that "it's fun when you screw up".

His father is empirical, analytical, "intimidatingly intelligent", and poor at expressing emotion, but because the parents had divorced when our artist was two years old, he has been less important in his life than the stepfather—a sculptor. The stepfather has certainly influenced him in the aesthetic direction and taken him to museums, and been a good friend in spite of some differences. His mother is, however, the person he has been really close to. She looms so large that he at first has a hard time beginning to talk about her, but when he does he says that she is very intelligent and extremely emotional: she loves children, knows how to relate to them at different ages, and is centered on family life. She invests a lot in her friends and has kept several since grade school. In all these matters the artist identifies with her: "I used to be the spitting image of her … she taught me intuitive social skills, things that no one would ever tell you."

He sees himself as a very emotional person, one who expresses his emotions on the spot. As for anger, he tends to bottle it up, and in this he has the model of his stepfather, who tends to release his anger—and "he's very aggressive"—too late and in inappropriate ways. So it is the availability of emotions, not specifically anger, that connect him with the other artists in this group, and that connect with his painting; for he also writes, and there he has to be organized, while when he paints he responds to the encouragement to be completely spontaneous.

Whirlwinds, equally fuzzy except for a kind of eye in the storm surrounding the house in the lower left, was done by a young woman who took the part of her personality that relates to art from her father, not her mother. She is one of the two people in this cluster who are not artists themselves. She starts her image work in the corners, which she flips and smudges and darkens, but preserves the house and its immediate surroundings within a protective circle. Shortly after completing the image she tells us that it could be "the wizard's house surrounded by tornadoes, but it does have a path out, the little path that goes off to the side", and connects that with her present precarious living situation: her mother may sell the house they live in and leave her homeless. She also thinks about her father's house, "which is a one-bedroom cabin … and it's about the size of that little … it's in fact a little smaller than that."

This openness to her most immediate concerns as a source of her art comes from her very spontaneous father, who was "always goofy, with a lot of energy," a spontaneous man with an attitude that says "just go for it and don't care what happens and deal with it as you go". He now writes poetry, does watercolors, and builds houses. Her mother is more flighty and anxious—and has in fact never done the mothering in the household; that was something the father took on, as he took on the cooking and cleaning when the mother decided to take a job. The parents are divorced now, and she can see some resemblance in herself to both parents; she lives with her mother, however, having become a mother to her in turn by doing the shopping, the cooking, and the laundry. She sees her father regularly, sometimes at the poetry readings he holds at his house.

She describes herself as emotionally expressive, crying easily ("even at cat food commercials"), and tells us that she is particularly moved when she sees two people expressing compassion for each other. In this she resembles most of the artists in this group, but there is also an admixture of anger present: she recollects that when her mother got a new boyfriend she did not approve of, and failed to tell her father, she (our artist) bought two pounds of spaghetti which she broke into pieces and scattered on the floor. The image she has made, we conclude as she continues talking, is also a reminder of childhood feelings: she recalls that in one of the houses where she and her parents lived her bedroom was on the bottom floor, next to the basement, and "it was such a lonely place, way down at the bottom of the house for a kid, … coyotes always howling out there … ." We may say that without the benefit of artistic training and habits, she could discover the expressive power of smudging purely in her strong feelings about the subject.

Perceptions of an Inner World is, for all its apparent similarity, differently made. Its author, the other nonartist in this group, warned us from the start that she would work in a repetitive kind of way. She then constructed much of her image by duplicating several flowers and setting them out here and there, thereby filling up the space, and then changed most of the colors in the picture by overlaying the pink from the star-gazer lily onto the other flowers. Although she did a little smudging early, she confined it to the center of the lily and only later did she move toward the rest of the picture. She moved back and forth between duplicating, smudging, and darkening, filled up every last bit of space, and result is dense and close. In this sense the image is different from the others in the cluster.

Not only was the image differently made, but it also stands for a different psychological process. We do not find in her an openness to emotion; she reports, with understandable sadness, that neither of her parents showed affection or accepted it from her, or was in any other way very communicative. The parents never seemed close to each other either, and everyone in the family essentially went his own way. This is very different from how she would like to be, so she has sought therapy; she is attempting to be able to accept affection in relationships and to cultivate her emotions. "Emotions are everything who I am, my identity, my place in the world," she says, perhaps too willfully.

Our impression is that the emotions to which she is so open are mostly negative; affection is felt as something that she needs to receive but cannot give, while sadness and emptiness are close to the surface. She tells us that she is resentful of men and afraid of them, and tells us as well that she had been traumatized sexually as a child.[2] She is also recovering from a five-year intense but unfruitful relationship—a very freeing prospect, but also a lonely and confusing one. Through her therapy, and this new freedom, she feels that she is growing rapidly in independence, but she is also confused and lonely.

The image seems more to reflect the need to fill up her whole space, and to fill it evenly. I am reminded more forcefully than with most of our artists that her image making resembles her speech pattern: it is voluble and even in tone, neither modulated nor emphatic, nor distinguishing between figure and ground. It is as if she could not relax, but had always to be doing or saying something. She volunteers her own interpretation of the image toward the end of the interview. The blurriness, she says, represents the confusion in her life; she had relied on the past relationship too much, and now is floating.

The young man who created **Split** returns us to image making that is dominated by anger, but the anger seems more avoidant than

---

[2] In this connection we might point out the focus on the star-gazer lily and the imposition of the color pink on the other flowers. We have seen among the participants of the previous chapter that the lily may be seen as inviting and threatening when it is connected with sexual abuse, and an evocation of this memory might lend urgency to dealing with the image.

engaged. We judge this in part from his abstract mode of proceeding: the heavy use of filters—which themselves are psychologically distant from the image—the satisfaction in nearly obliterating the image, the search for an adequate abstract expressiveness symbolized by words such as "dancy-dancy", "bleeding", and "plasma floating aimlessly". Toward the end he seems intent on—preoccupied, he says—splitting the image diagonally, and eventually he comments that he is different from his father, because his father likes pictures only if they look like something recognizable.

That is indeed a major theme in his recollections; his father has disappointed him repeatedly, and the first instance had to do with drawing. "The very beginning of my art making career was what I remember of being four years old ... . I picked up a pen and had a yellow legal pad and decided to draw my dad's car, and that's when I knew that I really liked drawing cars. I drew triangles, wheels, you know—whatever—just shapes, and I said, 'Dad, this is your car", and I drew eight really systematically, and I was meticulous. I thought, you know, this is a bumper—and it didn't look like a bumper but it was geometric forms—and my dad looked at it and said, "That's not my car", and put it down, and that's when I knew that I really liked art and I liked drawing."

Surely one brief experience does not explain one's future develop-ment, but our artist tells us of very uncommunicative parents—the father "psycho" and violent, the mother crabby and hard—whom he resents and would like to yell at now if he could. The parents manage to stay together by their interlocking needs, he says perceptively, and by the mother's denying the otherwise obvious fact that the father has a child by another woman. His ambition matches his anger: it is to be filthy rich and return all that his parents had given him.

Although his anger matches that of the artist who drew *Destitute Depot*, we think it would be a mistake to connect it with his art equally directly. Rather than showing us his family situation forcefully and locating himself within it, he chooses to portray it distantly: respond-ing to what he had seen as a split in the original image, he worked so as to preserve it and portray it abstractly. Although he makes no direct connection to his life, he tells us enough so that we can do so with con-fidence: the Catholic Church, he feels, has ruined his life and split his family up. It did so by enouraging the kind of hypocrisy and psycho-logical distance that he was the victim of. We might add that he is as split off from peers as he is from his parents—and, returning to his image, that its very abstractness is as much a symbol of the split as is the dividing line he sees there.

THE PSYCHOLOGICAL DYNAMICS OF
THIS CLUSTER

With two exceptions, then, these images have been made by individuals with highly available emotions, or at least the emotion of anger; *they seem to translate emotional energy directly into something to say and/or a vigorous graphic gesture to say it with.* If we are to speak of the pictures as maps of their makers' interpersonal space, it is a space where *an emotional parent and an organized parent join forces: the one provides the freedom of expression, while the other offers the encouragment of coherence.*

Two people proceeded somewhat differently: the one who made *Perceptions* used a style designed to fill her inner emptiness by filling the picture's space, yet betraying her momentary confusion at the same time, while the one who made the *Split* picture portrayed, in his hands-off abstractness, his angry withdrawal from his family.

I can now return to two painters to whom I had given short shrift in anticipation of a more detailed discussion; they have given us particularly rich protocols and nicely flesh out the complex dynamics that motivate them.

SCREAM

The young man of twenty-one years whom I shall call Howard and who created this picture begins his work with one habit—that of drawing faces to express how he is feeling—and one dominant feeling about the day of testing (which he recollects only later)—his reaction to the destruction in Sarajevo which he had heard about on the radio that morning. He chooses to work with the Village picture, and, as he would have predicted, draws several faces on the castle wall, duplicating them and integrating them carefully into the wall. None of what we will see in the final image will be prefigured by the first several interventions. He draws a colossal figure lying across the whole canvas, its arms encircling the castle, and then, choosing one of the windows of one of the houses as a discrete unit, he multiplies it many times across the canvas, either stretched out across the top edge or bunched against the upper right corner. We do not understand what he is doing and when we ask him, he does not either. As he works, however, the meaning begins to emerge: he asks how many nations there are in the United Nations. The number of multiplied windows is intended to correspond to that, and this in turn refers to his thinking about Sarajevo.

Figure 40. Scream

Now Howard stops: "this is too sad for me: it doesn't fit my mood." He introduces some vivid reds to lighten the mood, but that does not work either. "It's all gone to hell", he says. (It might be said parenthetically that working from one's mood of the moment is no guarantee of consistency: the mood may in itself be complex, and satisfying one pole of the mood may bring out the other: his sadness and wish for happiness, for example cannot both be satisfied at the same time.) He starts over with the original Village, works quickly, draws the figure from Edvard Munch's *The Scream*, adds a van Gogh figure (curiously strait-jacketed), and is done.

Talking with us right after finishing the picture, Howard mentions first his interest in Munch's and van Gogh's pain. Volubly and somewhat indirectly, he talks about the artist's personality and wonders how anyone could be so tormented as to want to kill himself. He does not mention it being an issue with him, but does see its relevance to his "anxieties about people being happy, or myself being happy … . I am always worrying about my friends getting their crap together, and … part of it's from [the fact that] I don't want to clean it up after them. Because a lot of people are really irresponsible." He goes on to recall van Gogh's period as a preacher, when he thought he would become closer with people but could not, and then his isolation as a painter. Howard's own work as a photographer is isolating, because in doing it "you put yourself apart from others".

We note that his speaking style is meandering and voluble, but that it is always perceptive; his words flow without prior selection, and describe a person gappling with the issues of pain, isolation and protectiveness. Talking about his switching from one way of doing the image to another, he says, "my mind works a lot in those ways in that I have got a lot on my mind and I am thinking about a lot every day, and reading the newspapers you go from article to article, you have this broad spectrum of interest, and then you pick an endeavor in a certain area you care about, so I always like to have a general knowledge of everything and then a specific knowledge of things I am most interested in—yeah, I did that Yugoslavia thing and then I just dropped it, you know."

His family is very close; one might say, enmeshed. His father could always do a lot of his work at home, so they were always close physically as well as emotionally. "He was really active with me, we'd play baseball together." Now they have a good relationship, one in which they can discuss pretty much anything. It is his relation to his mother, however, that adds the complexity we would expect. He introduces the topic by indirection, and the indirection reveals more than a direct plunge might:

> As my dad became more successful my mom took a stronger role, because
> my grandparents had lived with us since I was one—my maternal grand-
> parents. So she was always taking care of them, because her father had been
> ill since she was in college. He was mobile, he was fine, but he had health
> problems. So did my grandmother. So it was nice of my father to let them
> live with us, but it was really a big benefit to my sister and me, I felt ... . He
> was a draftsman, so that's where I got my inspiration. He'd teach me how to
> draw things anytime I asked.

The grandparents' eventual death helped set in place a part of
Howard's developing character. He became very protective of his
younger sister who, coincidentally, became much more mature herself.
"When my grandfather died it taught me that, well, it was my first touch
with mortality. So I saw myself taking this role where my mom was
providing for my grandfather, but I was the support for my mom I
look a lot like my mom, so I've always felt more in touch with her. But
as I grow older I start to look more like my father, so I don't know what
the deal is. But that made me grow up. It was a point where I decided
that I had to change some things, like get serious with school first of
all ... . So, being a small family, we're really close knit. So I see these
things as stepping stones, or definite markers that somehow coincide
correctly or incorrectly, for that matter."

Howard returns to the closeness that developed between him and
his mother when we discuss the expression of emotions in the family:
"When my grandmother died, I just felt like I had to be there for my
mom. I felt closer to my mom at that point than my dad was ... . She
needed her time to cry; that was a real growing point." This led to an
acute sensitivity to others that he shares with her now: "My mom and
I are both really concerned with everything, with other people, like
how they are feeling and what is going on in their lives. It used to
inhibit me more when I was younger, because I would be so concerned
with other people that I wouldn't think about *me* very often ... . When
I saw my mom cry, I'd cry."

In relation to his peers now, Howard is not dissimilar: a little too
accepting for his own good of the greater selfishness of others, but also
much in demand by women as a listener. "They finally think they have
someone to talk to, ... and then sometimes people will divulge things
to me that I don't think I should know at that moment, or that soon ... .
Mind you", he adds, "women who are attracted to me always have
older brothers."

This description of Howard may seem to have taken us quite far
away from the putative subject of his painting, *Scream*. We see him as

an unusually sensitive man, one with very open boundaries to others and few defenses against his own feelings. Not all feelings have an equal claim on him; it is pain that he seems most ready to feel. Protective of his mother and sister, he is perhaps ultimately protecting himself, but the protection takes the form of going out and meeting the pain head on through his art work. Well accustomed since childhood to doing art, and well practised in its techniques, he can grapple with his feeling of the moment, consider their opposites, efface everything he has done, and return—to Munch's *Scream* and van Gogh's pain.

HONEYMOON

The distance between a scream and a picture of a honeymoon seems great, but in matters of the emotional openness and closeness to family that underlie its making, it is in fact quite small. Dagmar is a senior art student who volunteered for the study in order to learn more about Photoshop and receive the feedback we were offering. In the session after the tutorial, she sets to work with energy and purpose. She is attracted to the green/red color opposition in the Garden picture and will work with complementary oppositions as much as she can, here choosing the colors for her work from the original photograph itself. The first purpose, however, is not the one she will discover as she works; as always, she thinks about the picture beforehand, and here she decides (as she tells us later) to redesign the picture geometrically, creating a space of color. In fact, there is a core of fantasy in this abstract intention: "I just wanted to make this inner space, like a window to look into the room." We presume that she herself does not know who is looking where and at what, or by what imaginative leap she had transformed an outdoor picture into a potential view inside.

She abstracts much of the space around the leaves by creating a grey-violet flat pattern which eventually becomes the wall that we see, and draws a large brown object on the right that looks to her like an owl. Looking at it some more, she begins to transform it into a chair—and with this transformation the future direction of the process seems set. "The chair seemed to demand this sort of space to sit in, so I added the table to give it company." Working rapidly, using only the stylus and the short, loose strokes that we see, she shades the table and the vase, adds a floor, and draws an electrical outlet. She says right then that it "adds a little reality to this pleasant picture."

Surely one of the remarkable things about this proces is that much of it was determined unconsciously, and that Dagmar followed an

Figure 41. Honeymoon

intention that she could not be aware of. The very reversal of the direction of looking—into a room rather than out of it—must have implied what would be seen, and surely the transformation of a blockish owl into a lacy chair was not merely a visual pun nor some distant free association: for when she is done, she does not hesitate to tell us that the chair had been bought by her parents on their honeymoon, and *Honeymoon* is the name by which the picture will be known.

In the question period that followed right after, she gives the picture two possible, compatible meanings. It looks flat to her, "kind of like a fake wallpaper, it's nice because it's crisp, but the red and blue seem to work nicely together", and this reminds her of her grandmother's attachment to wallpaper. The mix of textures in the wallpaper seems like a mix of cultures, too, with the flowers looking Japanese, "and how we absorb different ideas of what is beautiful and how we want to create that space with those beautiful things and acquire the things". When she adds that the electrical plug is a willful intrusion into this old-style beauty, she moves imperceptibly back toward the meaning she has revealed already: "you have these aesthetic things and then this reminder of what we have to do, like if it's a clock attached to that electrical plug, well ... the title is *Honeymoon*, and I guess you've always got something else to do—life isn't just a honeymoon."

What keeps her and her art so close to her parents' history, and what accounts for the self-assured style? Summarizing her art-making experience, she gives us a partial answer, revealing at once an attachment to art and to her father. "Well, my dad is a graphic designer, so growing up I always had lots of supplies to work with, and it was common for me to be painting or drawing. You know, as early as I could pick up a tool. So all the way through early childhood until now, art has been something that I just did."

The father was, then, very affectionate and playful, and would take his only child out on excursions; they would go walking or bicycling, and "if it was outdoors, it was with my dad." An energetic man who liked to solve problems, make things work better, and question the usual ways of doing them, he provided a model she has followed closely. Her mother was practical and responsible, working full time but ensuring that Dagmar was taken care of—a description which is certainly positive but lacking somewhat in warmth. The parents separated when she was five and divorced when she was twelve, and then felt quite differently about further contact: the father wanted to remain close but the mother wanted no contact at all. This was hard for Dagmar: "I felt a sense of loyalty to my mom, wanting her to be happy, but also knowing that it was really important for me to be with my dad because I loved to be with him." Now, some ten years later, she tries to keep some distance from her, finding her too dependent, but remains close to her father.

He in turn is close to her. "Well, my dad gave me the chair. This was four years ago, I had moved out of my mother's house and was living on my own. My dad drove up with some of the furniture I had in my old bedroom, and he brought up this red chair—it was his chair from their honeymoon. He just kept it safe, and so he brought it up because he knew I always loved it, and that's how it came to be mine."

Dagmar's picture is, then, testimony to her closeness with her father, and to the wish—not an identical one—for a closeness between the parents themselves. But it is style and mode of working, not merely the subject, that we need to understand; after all, cluster 6, also composed of artists, will show a comparable desire for unification but use a different approach to do so. Here—with Dagmar as well as with the whole cluster—the mode of working is gestural, and the pictures are unified not by a formal vision but by an accumulation of gestures.

Like the others, Dagmar makes it a point to say that she is emotional. "I am a really emotional person, like I totally empathize if I see something sad, like in someone else's life, or in a movie, or on television." And it is the capacity to feel emotion, rather than let others know about it, that connects to her free style: "You know, I'll have all these emotions come up, but for myself, it's hard for those emotions to come through". Where love is concerned she seems more puzzled and overwhelmed by its intensity than afraid of expressing it: "Love—it's just really intense, it's just really amazing, and you know, I still haven't figured it out … . I don't know how to explain it." And where anger is concerned, she expresses it as clearly as she feels it: "I know that I have a lot of anger inside me because, you know, if my cat does something, I'll get *really* pissed, and it's just my cat!"

I have said about the artists in this cluster that they seem to translate emotional energy directly into something to say as well as vigorous graphic gestures with which to say it. We shall see a more formal way of making images, by equally trained artists, in cluster 6 (Chapter 8); the difference between them, it will become clear, will be in the degree of their emotional sublimation.

CHAPTER 6

Fourth Cluster

Dense Paintings and Relentless Control

Let us look at the images that make up this cluster and describe them first without reference to the cluster analysis. All seem dense and closely assembled, most use some black, while a few are layered in strata; the strata either remain distinct or interweave. Whether the final product remains clearly readable or obscure, there is a sense of complexity or of piling up; one's gaze is not invited to move across the surface of the image by dynamic lines or into space by deep recession. Some of the images are made up of repetitive elements which by themselves suggest an obsessive process, and one picture maker in fact writes his message out in words and repeats it throughout in different type sizes. There seems little evidence anywhere of the painters' hands; rather, the images seem cut up, assembled, multiplied, blurred, or transformed in their texture or color by the sophisticated electronic tools of the software. The photograph which served as the starting point has been for the most part obliterated, having served only as a starting point, perhaps even an excuse, for the work which the person "really" wanted to do.

The images do seem coherently grouped, then. In terms of the work done by the cluster analysis program, they were very high on the *saccadic* factor, which reflects a start-and-stop process, sharp outlines, and static composition, and to a lesser but interesting degree, a dense effect and a mechanical mode of working. The cluster is also described by the *boldness* factor, which reflects a noted boldness of attempt and final effect, a clearly evoked emotional response on the raters' part, and an idiosyncratic conception of the image. In looking at the images again we can see the boldness in the many blacks and the frequent red/blacks; and the images do seem to call insistently for some sort of response from the viewer. Idiosyncracy is harder to describe in its own terms; it is relative to all the images that were produced for us, and can be judged by the reader only after looking at the whole set, something which I am happy to recommend.

The reader will see, I hope, a clear dynamic operating: all these individuals will appear highly controlled, even relentlessly driven, and all but one will have a core issue which will require a persistent exercise of the control.

THE PSYCHOLOGICAL PROCESS SEEN INDIVIDUALLY

As before, we shall see first whether the individual interpretations we had made of our painters create a coherent pattern. ***Banshees***, then, made by a man in his late thirties, impressed us (among other qualities) by its meticulous work, its "hands-off" use of filters and the layered multiplication of their effects, the desire to create a frightening effect, and finally the experimenter's sense that the individual—however complex, thoughtful, and precise in his expression—had evaded making an emotional connection which would allow her to "feel" his presence and artistic purpose. One of our interpretive comments at the time was that there was one theme which underlay his many obvious strengths, and that was the intensity of his one fear: that of dying a violent, ugly, unaesthetic death. He did tell us that his dreams were scary and that they involved death; yet he likes them, because when

Figure 42. Banshees

Figure 43. War of the Leaves

Figure 44. Garden Tools

Figure 45. Untitled with Flowers

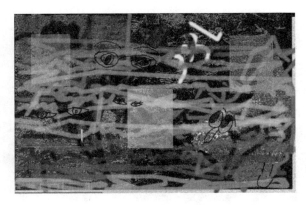

Figure 46. Graffiti

Figure 47. Lost

Figure 48. Textural Abyss

he wakes up from them he knows that he has survived them. We can connect the density of his work with the inexorable presence of this fear, and we may suppose that this engagement with image making serves to master the fear. He had chosen the photograph of the Village because it had a bit of the sinister quality that he needed so much to master.

War of the Leaves was produced by a man in his twenties, and it carries a clear, aggressive message; indeed he says, perhaps too blandly, that he "hates leaves" and "likes to destroy sceneries". The image was produced predominantly by mechanical repetition and resembles a cartoon, as if the violence were thereby contained and pushed away to a safe distance. He recalls his adolescent liking for comic book art, and in a frank and amiable way speaks of his aggressive imagery; yes, the image is aggressive, he says, but none of this matters very much. To us the style seems distant, intellectualized—as does his style of speaking— yet it is also connected with his clear awareness of aggressive intent and his pervasive negative stance toward his parents. We learn later that, the distant style notwithstanding, he feels responsible for his parents' divorce, and we begin to ask whether that sense, combined with his dislike for the parents, is not central to his organization; it seems to us to require constant control over his aggressive feelings (admitted to us and himself only as thoughts, not as feelings). That strong feelings underlie the imagery and demand expression is proved by his request to make a second image, which he makes quickly and uses for a direct message: in *This Could Have Been Us* he simply paints a mushroom cloud which wreaks indiscriminate destruction.

Garden Tools is a picture produced by a young man who, it seems, also has one overriding matter to control. His image is crowded, assembled on a grid, and overlaid by sentences and phrases which came to him early in the process of working. The words are about the environment, but what leaps to the eyes are the two orange phrases "tools working to control" and "managing nature". The visual style, then, is dense and repetitive and the verbal message is about control; and our inclination to see it as obsessive is confirmed by the young man, who tells us that he had "all these words floating around in my head". The overriding early issue concerns his family's chaotic emigration to the US; for years they were split up and poor and he had to learn to rely on himself. "When I was small everybody was having such a hard time coping with everything and my mom was having to work very hard ... you took care of your problems yourself." It seems that if he has a strong need to control his environment, we can understand where it would come from.

An even denser picture was produced by a man in his late twenties. **Psychedelic Village** is a collage of fragments superimposed on the Village photograph, and it was chosen because it would be a safe, happy place to live; some of the elements superimposed on it came from the Flowers picture, which is very colorful, and the tutorial picture Temple, which the man insisted on using as well and which offered his work a spiritual cast. The "psychedelic" aspect is meant to be happy and free, yet the image, which is admittedly colorful, also seems heavy and resolute. We learn from him that he has dealt all his life with loss of control—alcoholism, adolescent psychosis, and a bipolar disorder—and have come to understand, as he does, that he has a persistent need to keep his life in order; and we can see that need as perfectly justified. To give a fuller account of his complex character, we shall return to him at greater length.

The young man who was content to call his image **Untitled with Flowers** also started with the Village photograph, but constructed his picture more through repetitive operations than with a definable goal in mind. He copied patterns from within the photograph and repro-duced them several times, and created an abstract, key-like pattern in light brown which he copied in different colors, oriented this way and that, and set down repeatedly. Admittedly, creating through process rather than plan is consistent with the work of an art student, but his need to fill the whole surface is his own: under magnification he fills all the holes left in the image by the assembled patches. (He even puts a tiny black figure into the very center of the picture, as if to establish his own presence in it.) The result is aesthetic at the same time as it is close and airless. An inhibited young man, all his life a helper in his father's tile (!) business, he failed to grow up to become the sportsman and fisherman his father had been, and became more like his mother, polite and anxious, and somewhat like his older and dominating sister, who was the "ultimate neat freak". He has, however, come to identify with his father's authority, having "gotten over" his "little rebellion" and come to appreciate him again. His style of relating to the inter-viewer is good-humored but distant and intellectual; he reasons things out rather than feeling them, and makes clear that he is planful, not spontaneous.

Not all the dense images were produced by men: **Graffiti**, for example, was produced by a woman in her early twenties, and is equally layered, equally impenetrable, and not a little aggressive in its scribblings over the original Hillside landscape. Although its colors are happier, its mood is not: big, adult eyes look down upon childlike eyes. She explains that the picture is about "multinational corporations, all the people in their ignorance looking up and being scared". We learn from her that her parents were demanding and even denigrating and competitive, and that she has in many ways been oversocialized; her father in particular was somewhat of a martinet who insisted on keeping everything in perfect order. Still an important figure in her life—she sees him as still attached to her, though we may presume that the attachment is mutual—he now appears in the picture as well: the multinational corporations "could be my dad and also the government", and "maybe in a way it looks like everything is under control, everything is civilized, but it really isn't". Quite unemotional in her speech, she, too seems obsessive in her style and concerned with control. Having been controlled to excess by her father, she now maintains her own control through an inhibited exterior and allows some feelings to be symbolized by obliteration.

Winterland, also produced by a woman in her early twenties, has an aesthetic intent, but it is not a happy picture: the harmony is mustard yellow and dull raspberry and the space is crowded with additional trees and buildings. She calls the colors "funky" and sees a dyspeptic cast in them when she calls the pink a "Pepto-Bismol paint". The daughter of emotionally distant parents, she, too, sees a central issue in her life: depression. She copes with it with relentless drive: she hopes never to slack off, never to get stuck in a depression rut, and live up to her mother's expectation to be "tenacious, to not give up; quitters never win, winners never quit." We shall reserve a fuller discussion of her for the end of the chapter.

The picture called *Lost* is made dense, too, but by a different technique. The young woman who created it selected small elements of the photograph Garden, without further modification, and replicated them in tight clusters over the whole surface of the image; in this way, she made a very evenly textured canopy of leaves hang above a stepwise path leading back into the picture and flanked by two patches of rhythmically regular grass. She transformed the original disorder of the garden into order, albeit at the price of much repetition and an absence of breathing space. I think we can account both for the sense of being lost and for the order. As a child, she moved around a lot with her family, following her father's changes of jobs, and found this a source of insecurity; as she puts it, it had been rocky back and forth. This is exacerbated at the moment by her being a senior, as she tells us right after making the image, and "being completely lost." She is a perfectionist, like her organized and thrifty father, and enjoys working within imposed limits such as those provided by the image. The sense of being lost within those peregrinations and the need for order seem to strengthen each other.

All these individuals, both men and women, have told us of a dominant issue that requires a persistent application of their organizing abilities, and we were as impressed with the presence of such an issue as we were with the need for order—a need which here is no less than obsessive. The next person is, however, less easy to understand; although we find an admitted perfectionism in him as in the others, we do not see it directed toward a single issue or even a group of issues. The maker of *Textural Abyss*, a young man, does describe himself as perfectionistic and as protective of his perfectionistic but ineffectual father who was tyrannized by his own, wealthy father, and he does see himself as too even-keeled, too unemotional, too inexpressive. When making his picture he felt blocked throughout and tried various devices in hopes of finding one that would produce something satisfactory; one of them was intended to engage his emotions—spray painting the walls of the temple in the tutorial photograph—and perhaps betrayed a barely discernible rebellion against authority. We do find him unusually even in his tempo and unexcitable, and perhaps this style is enough to account for the steady and thick accumulation of effects in the picture; but if the style has psychodynamic underpinnings, we have not discovered what they are.

THE PSYCHOLOGICAL DYNAMICS OF THIS CLUSTER

Nevertheless, when we combine these individual interpretations we do see a clear dynamic operating: all these individuals are highly controlled, even obsessive, and all but one have a core issue which requires a persistent exercise of the control. Among these is a feeling of being driven by sex, in some cases combined with distance from people, in others combined with needing to manage the distance continuously.

The makers of *Banshees, War of the Leaves*, and *Psychedelic Village* all describe themselves as being driven, or having been driven, by the need for lots of sex, at the same time as they were unable or unwilling to be intimate; the makers of *Winterland, Garden Tools* and *Textural Abyss* find sex very important but seek an intense love as well, speaking of love as a kind of ideal absolute which they wish to find. The maker of *Lost*, while saying that sex is not all that important, finds love vital—and she adds, "some people have religion; love is my thing in life". It seems to us to matter little whether the striving is principally for sex or for love; what matters is the feeling of being driven. In this respect the subjects are as compulsive as in their ordered style they were obsessive.

Only the makers of *Untitled with Flowers* and *Graffiti* are at the moment inhibited sexually and not fully open to intimate relationships; the one overidentifies with his father while the other seems too emotionally close to hers, which may well inhibit the sexual compulsiveness seen in some of the others. But like them, they are obsessive in their cognitive style.

One is left with the dilemma all psychodynamic theorists face: whether to emphasize the defensive style of the person or the needs that call for its constant use. In all but two people we have seen both, while in two we have seen the obsessive style only. Surely it will seem prudent to presume that the two normally require each other and when working together will affect the art-making style most clearly. Be that as it may, what leaps to the eyes is overdetermination; many needs, experiences and fantasies are connected by a few common meanings, and the latter can be revealed both in the image making and the subsequent interviews. The notion of a group's style, such as the "dense style" here, is necessary if we are to go beyond the individual, but it remains an abstraction achievable only at the cost of some simplification. Our knowledge does begin with the whole individual and it is to two individuals that we return.

PSYCHEDELIC VILLAGE

The man we will call Harry volunteered for this study in part because he wanted to help out with the research—he had known me as a student—in part for self-knowledge. To me he was a serious student with clearcut goals, and to several of the research assistants, who also knew him, he was a delightful acquaintance with a quirky sense of humor. He was also known for his openness about himself, so we broke our rule about taking on people we knew and worked with him. He made his picture with an assistant he knew, but his interview was conducted by someone unknown to him; at the end, when he came in for the feedback on his results, we found ourselves as analytic with him as he had been open with us and felt pleased to have included him.

Starting by saving blocks from several of the original photographs, with the clear intention of integrating them with the village picture as a base and creating a "psychedelic village", he started pasting his image together. "Psychedelia" is a state of mind he had been in, sometimes bad, but "it can be a good thing, too; it can be a vision into a different state of being, where there is not as much routine, defense, fear—stuff like that." Elements from the Temple picture provided

Figure 49. Psychedelic Village

a spiritual aspect, flowers added color, and village was a safe, nice, happy place to live. To integrate the blocks at their edges he smudged their borders gently, and then to give the picture an interesting appearance he would adjust its hues and contrasts and use one or more of the filters available in Photoshop; the filter "posterize" in particular gave him a somewhat raw, abstract quality. He made himself noticed to the experimenter by little quirks such as changing the numerical parameters of the filters—something most people were unaware of, let alone cared about. By the time he had finished he had used none of the hand tools. The result of his many pastings and filterings was both striking and dense.

In the interview he talked freely about his parents and himself. His father, a depressed alcoholic when Harry was growing up, was abusive and withdrawn and only recently has been put on appropriate medication. Harry does have several points in common with his father— the way he laughs and jokes around, for example—and on the whole accepts them, proud to emulate his father in some ways. In one major way he wishes he were different, and that is his own alcoholism. I shall return to this presently.

Harry's mother has been a wallflower all her life, with no friendships outside the family, and correspondingly protective, loving and close to Harry; even now their relationship is warm and trusting and they talk to each other on the phone every week. Even working forty hours and week and going to college, she would find time to make breakfast and put everyone's towels in the laundry so they would be warm after their shower. When Harry was a child she was also protective of his father, which, given his alcoholism, amounted to supporting his habit, but in that regard she is now firmer. She is bright, taught Harry to read when he was little, and is still the one to pressure him to do things right. She's characterized as playful—in fact, the whole family is playful, and "there were a lot of goofy things we would do."

Discipline was inconsistent and Harry's procrastination and lack of self-discipline comes from that. If Harry hadn't picked up after himself it might go unnoticed, or his father might fly into a rage for an hour—he simply never knew in advance; his friends could not understand why he was always trying to plan out all the alternative ways of responding to his father depending on his mood when returning from work. In turn, Harry believes he put his mother through the same sort of hell his father put her through—with his alcoholism, he drove her crazy.

If playfulness and support were the bright sides of family life, then alcoholism was the scourge. Harry himself began to drink in high school and this, bad enough in itself, exacerbated a condition he did not even know he had: a bipolar disorder. As a drinker he did not relate closely to his peers and with women had only one-night stands; as a drinker in what he came to know as the manic phase of his disorder he could become delusional. Once during one of his crazy spells his parents kicked him out of the house and he began obsessing about making love with a girl and founding a new race of people; it was an apocalyptic vision which got him arrested and (mis)diagnosed as schizophrenic. Psychotic he was, in the manic swing of the bipolar disorder, but that was diagnosed only later and in the meantime his high school years were marked by several stays in mental institutions. He did not sober up until he was 21.

Like his father before him, when Harry was 15 he joined Alcoholics Anonymous. AA has become a center in his life and its philosophy a pervasive guideline, and in fact Harry has made it much more important than his father had. While the father was spiritual now and then, and left self-help books lying around the house, Harry's spirituality is deep and he looks to it for fulfillment; he does retreats and workshops, goes to different churches, and prays every day. He believes in a loving God, not a punishing one, and believes that he is on earth now because he was chosen to be here, probably sometime before he was born; this is consistent with his belief in reincarnation with a choice. He is in school in order to pursue a career leading to private, clinical practice, doing spiritual emergence work.

This system of controls may seem strong but we must remind ourselves that it was erected against a massive loss of control. The example of his father and his own adolescent drinking might have been quite enough, but he also suffered from a bipolar disorder. More than that: he also suffered a bout with cancer—whose details we did not ask about—which required a massive operation about which he remembers that his body was opened up and then put back together. Whatever the details of the operation, it is his image of being put back together that seems so poignant a symbol for his need for total renewal. He has suffered much more than most at his age and emerged strong—perhaps buttressed by his defenses and his constantly supported goals and beliefs. Nor are his defenses without their flexibility; we have mentioned his quirky sense of humor and the affection in which the research assistants who knew him felt for him.

Not only are his defenses voluminous, if we may so put it, but a few of them are downright obsessive. (Both qualities seem important for understanding the style and substance of his image.) When speaking of his relationships he mentioned that he has always been somewhat strange in that area: in high school he had lots of sex in one-night stands and would then obsess about his women all the time. His present needs are broader—he includes affection, beauty, the ability to discuss things, mental and physical health—but he can still add with mock heavy breathing, "lots and lots of sex", and resuscitate his earlier ideal of "me and this penthouse pet who is smart and is a massage expert and has a huge trust fund." In fact, he is quite monogamous now and is engaged to be married.

I am trying to explain the *denseness* and the *assembled quality* of his image. I turn to the massive kind of reconstruction that he has performed here and readily see in it his need to control a threat of a massive loss of control; likewise, the patient filling in of all the space seems similar to his obsessive defense. Density and repetition seem the particular qualities of his picture and they find their origins in his personality—just as, had I devoted comparable space to the maker of *Banshees*, I would have discussed his complex *layering of filters* which resembles his personal complexity and the layers of defenses that he says he puts between himself and emotions.

But I need to explain the attempt at *lightness* here as well, and the hands-off nature of his work with the software program. To him the term psychedelic is light because it means happy, joyful, and free; he has had psychedelic experiences and we presume they have been good on the whole, and now he can connect them to an ultimate kind of security, the knowledge that you will not die and that things will be taken care of. For all the wish to give up control to a more secure universe, he also retains some distance from people ("I want friends in some ways but I don't want to do what I have to do to get them,") and this seems enough to explain the distant, *hands-off*, mode of transforming the image. Our *Banshees* painter had been asked about this more directly and agreed, as we have seen, that the hands-off filters were a way of keeping himself at a distance.

The next painter has produced an equally dense image but by somewhat different means and in response to somewhat different concerns. An art student with a sure sense of technique, "Diana" is in many ways as driven as Harry though less distant from people, and by her aesthetic concerns and her own version of compelling controls she helps us flesh out the meaning of this style in her own clear and thoughtful way.

WINTERLAND

Starting with the Village photograph as well—a photograph the painters have come to see as suggesting a family constellation in its dominating castle and dependent houses—Diana started by outlining some of the windows and pasting copies of them here and there. She then lost interest in them and started changing some of the colors; she turned the sky red, to complement the green grass, and tried other hues here and there, never quite satisfied with them. Her feelings about the beginning of her work were betrayed by comments such as "I should mix it with yellow to make it look like someone peed on it," and "it reminds me of the Grinch that stole Christmas," and "who would have ever thought I'd be using pink and green—those are such yucky colors." By trial and error more than by plan, she tried various effects, including those produced by many of the hands-off filters, examined them and either accepted or rejected them. In this way she thickened the thin space: she placed trees where there were none, added clouds (and most often removed them), and balanced the lower right corner of the picture with a heavy house copied from left center.

This last decision was as stylistic as it was aesthetic. To do this she drew careful outlines, one at a time, around the trees and around the house, and selected them out for copying and pasting where she wanted them. She poured color here and there, burgundy into the sky and her Pepto-Bismol pink into the sunny sides of the houses, and divided the castle from the houses by a kind of fluffy snow which she soon dirtied. We have no explanation for some of these details, but one small peculiarity does call for attention: the careful placement of minute windows into some of the bushes. (They are not visible in the image reproduced, unfortunately, because it was compressed when saved, and loses much of its detail when printed.) She found her direction only as she worked, which is to say that her sense of direction came from a tenacious application, and eventual acceptance, of a mode of working.

Talking about her picture afterwards, she was not quite happy with it: some of the colors didn't go well together, she says, and the yellowish clouds took away from the whiteness. She did accept the dark mood, however, saying that "there is a dark side to every artist; ... my moods fluctuate a lot; I am very moody ... and my art has been bringing that out lately." As to the attraction of the Village picture, she said only that it "offered a distant point of view: there was more to work with." It turns out later that, in our view, her parents' critical standards, and at least her father's emotional distance, were suggested by the forbidding, tall buildings.

Unlike Harry, Diana is not overtly distant from people but does make the *management of distance* an issue; in fact, it is her relentless attention to it that connects her dynamic with the others in this group.

Figure 50. Winterland

Distance is indeed the theme of her relation to her father: in a few words she says, "I don't talk to him as a friend; he's very distant from me. He had a hard life when he was young and I think as a result of that he's very reclusive; ... like not saying hello to me when I come in the house is the normal kind of thing." She was not exactly afraid of him when she was young, but did not feel safe around him either: "he used to tickle me till I cried ... and to this day I can't be tickled; I will flip out. I will literally start crying and just lose control ... . As far as my feelings go, he never expressed any feelings, he never told me he loved me." She does realize that he is responsible and supportive financially, and appreciates that he instilled good morals in her, "such as being diligent and tenacious." And yes, she does share some qualities with him, such as flying off the handle about small things, verbally abusing people close to her, and having a peculiar, punning sense of humor.

But she is also different from him, and her words on this subject seem somewhat terse: "I am extremely emotional. I am very one on one. I am very honest. I am very loving. I show it. I am a go-getter, like I go out and do things, and all he ever wants to do is watch TV." She attributes some of these qualities to her mother's example or teachings. Submissive to her husband when Diana was growing up, her mother discovered that she had been held back by society and rebelled, and now finds herself angry much of the time and quite distant from her husband. Yet it was she who taught her daughter about honesty, and it was she who was "direct and straightforward ... a go-getter, honest and open," "If I wanted to know about sex when I was a kid, she'd tell me. She treated me almost as if I was more of a friend than a daughter ... . So I grew up kind of as an adult, you know, I never really had that childhood. I was always around adults anyway."

Asked how she differs from her mother, Diana says that her mother works all the time and she doesn't have time to do anything else—she does the taxes, she does the bills, she does the accounts for her husband's business, the mortgage, the car and all the financial stuff. "She does it all, plus her work, plus other organizations that she works for. She is just constantly swamped." As she says this, Diana realizes that she is describing herself as well: "I guess in that way I am the same, because I have that quality of overdoing it and getting really overwhelmed." She does, in fact, identify with her mother and "probably the only difference that comes between us is that she was raised in a different era."

Diana has two models of relationships, then, a distant one from her father and a closer one from her mother, but the latter is not uncomplicated: the closeness was achieved at the cost of being treated as an adult. Nor is the mother markedly more stable than the father—she, too, is hypersensitive, and blows comments way out of proportion. (In Diana's life there was another older woman, a friend's mother, with whom Diana spent much time; she was "literally insane", polite in public but screaming bloody murder at the children at home. Diana sees it as her pattern to befriend female friends who had half crazy mothers.) She has both a model of distance and a model of risky affection.

We begin to understand why she would accept the goals that her parents held out for her. "To just be strong and follow my heart and what I want to do. That I be tenacious, that I not give up. Quitters never win, winners never quit." Tenaciousness, we think, would help bridge the gap between her cold father and herself and bind together some of the uncertainties in the warmer relation to her mother; it would also put the responsibility for making and maintaining contact squarely on her shoulders. Her own goals follow: "To just do as well as I can. To be excellent in what I do; excellence is really important to me. Just over-achieving, succeeding, doing whatever to be up on top of what I am doing. Aware. That I never slack off or get stuck in a depression rut."

And we begin to understand the needs that she brings to her intimate relationships. She is in fact in her first romantic and sexual relationship, and she is in it quite intensely. "This is my first relation-ship. I am a very faithful person. Once I started going out with Tom and ended up falling in love with him, I've just been with him. I haven't wanted to cheat. I'm not like that." She likes their sexual life on the whole but knows that there must be more: "you could be doing it and totally be in a trance; and I want that trance." She barely dated when she was in high school and is not sure whether that's because she was standoffish or whether there were very few men around (she did go to an all-girls school). In either case, relationships now are "extremely important. I think I am different from most people. I think relation-ships are everything. I think that friendships are everything. I think that life would be nothing without them. So I completely love relationships ... . I will put my everything into a friendship, for a really good friend. I would give them anything. And people find that really overwhelming."

Unlike most of the other individuals in this cluster, then, Diana does value closeness and openness ("I like to tell them about myself; I like to be really open"), but she seems to achieve it at the price of an unceasing, persistent dedication and effort. Her effort after closeness is in itself obsessive and she seems to give herself no respite from it. It is in her *driven style* that she resembles Harry and the other members of this group, whether they are merely obsessive, or obsessed with sex with or without intimacy; she is obsessed with relationships and in love with love. Asked whether she likes romantic movies or novels, she replies, "yes, I do. I like the juxtaposition between passion and romance. Some movies have just romance, some movies have both, and some movies are just passion, but I am really obsessed with passion."

I had mentioned that she began her picture by inserting little windows into the bushes. She did come up with an explanation, but this only suggested a further mystery to unravel. At first she pointed out the pun-like play on the images, a style of humor she shares with her father; then she spun out a fantasy: "it's pretty funny, a lot of people think of hiding in bushes and there is a window there and they're looking out into the world and the world can't see in. Like when you're inside your house and the house is dark inside. You can see out but no one can see you inside." Whatever specific meaning seeing without being seen may have for her, it also comments on the limits on intimacy with which she contends.

The "painters" here have compiled dense images with little breathing room. Their form resembles the painters' cognitive style and perhaps fulfills its needs: the painters seem driven and their defense is of the most driven kind, that is, obsessive. The images seem to vary in their emotional warmth, but they all symbolize some form of a struggle between warmth toward others and distance from them. Although distance from their parents appears as the grounds on which their dynamics are built, here I stress the defense: their pictures' density comes to be a symbol of an unrelenting—yet successful and not unproductive—defensive style.

CHAPTER 7

Fifth Cluster

Imposed Order, Inhibition, and the Acceptance of Parental Standards

Where the preceding cluster, the one with dense images, was driven and obsessive, the one we are coming to is inhibited, perfectionist, and in the grip of standards taken over from the parents.

But I am getting ahead of myself. The cluster is defined by images, and here they share three qualities: timidity, formality, and a saccadic style. The timid rating reflects our judgment that neither the process nor the final product ventured out, that the images did not evoke our emotional response, and that the content and form were banal—expectable and ordinary, revealing no specific idiosyncratic concerns. Formality, of course, was noted in an emphasis on organization, control, or subdivision. The third factor—a saccadic as opposed to a flowing process—indicated unconnectedness and hesitation during the picture making and a final product that was visually static or jagged. No other cluster approaches this one in its overall hesitations; cluster one was timid, too, but it expressed its compensatory longings forthrightly, and cluster four, though also saccadic, was driven and obsessive. Finally, cluster six, which will also be formal, will be informed by a flowing, skilled, and self-confident process.

If we look at the images afresh, we see them expressing an intense preoccupation with establishing order and balance; the pictures do not work by juxtaposition or tension, but by system. In four images the organizing principle is repetition. *Urbania* (see Figs. 51–59) depicts a looming, elongated building facing a tract of houses standing at attention row upon row, *Suburbia* transforms an informal village into a cookie cutter housing tract, *Framed Flowers* (see Fig. 60) not only creates

Figure 51. Urbania

Figure 52. Suburbia

Figure 53. Spectrum

Figure 54. The Persistence of Beauty

Figure 55. Waterfall

Figure 56. Wish You Were Here

Figure 57. Garden of Eden

Figure 58. Mine

Figure 59. Mieru

its borders by duplicating flowers but also arranges the borders concentrically, and *My Mother's Garden* (Fig. 61)—which is so little transformed from the original that it barely seems different—achieves its desired symmetry by multiplying the narcissus flowers.

In other pictures we see the imposition of a mechanical matrix: in *Spectrum* a mandala highlights the central persimmon, in *The Persistence of Beauty* the vase of flowers is overlaid with a matrix of geometric lines, in *Waterfall* a geometrically precise sun and its rays dominate and distract from a landscape that otherwise smoothly integrates a Sicilian and Burgundy countryside, and in *Wish You Were Here* flowers frame and prettify the village while bright red roofs ensure that we see it as happy. Two images achieve order by stating a binary opposition—the "his and hers" fruit of *Garden of Eden* and the childlike happy and sad faces of *Mine*. One image appears merely to decorate: in *Mieru* (Japanese for "I can see", explains its creator) the lily now has a curlicue, the flower petals are touched up, and the centers of other flowers have been accentuated with tiny dots of color (while an unexpected spot of something more primary erupts in the form of a bulging eye). Decorativeness itself is of course shared by most of the images, however differently it may have been achieved.

We are struck by some subtle and less easily described qualities as well. Several of the images seem created so as to hide something. They deflect our gaze from inquiring deeper, from seeing and sensing more, and perhaps while trying to discourage us only encourage us the more. Indeed, some of the pictures, rather than inviting a closer look, have eyes staring back at us or faces telling us to feel happy or sad, or windows that only reflect what is the outside without allowing a glimpse within. A sign in an illegible language, a title that needs translating in order to be understood, an intrusive accent of color that isolates a house from its surroundings, and a pretty rose overlaid with a dark, disturbing hole in the center—all seem to suggest, but not reveal, deeper private meanings.

Perhaps what strikes us most is that the images' expression is indirect or awkward. In some of them we sense a thin levity which we may not quite trust—the curlicue combined with the bulging eye in *Mieru*, the sad and happy faces framing a missing lily, for example—while in others we see an artificial imposition of structures which we cannot readily understand: for example, the words "his and hers" laid onto the persimmons, or the hard, geometric grids imposed on the leaves and flowers in *Spectrum* and *The Persistence of Beauty*.

Let me rephrase what it is we wish to understand. Of the three dimensions that define this cluster, we are inclined to see timidity and the saccadic process—and the peculiarly oblique modes of expression which struck us upon closer viewing—as aspects of an inhibition of emotional flow, and we suspect that these subjects' version of formality—the preoccupation with excessive or inappropriate ordering—is an attempt to impose standards upon a disorderly reality. If we look for what explains our artists' inhibition, and the sources of their need for order, we shall be maintaining the right focus.

THE PSYCHOLOGICAL PROCESS SEEN INDIVIDUALLY

Surely the most controlled of the images in this cluster is the first, **Framed Flowers** (Fig. 60). It is so unrelenting an example of order wrested from chaos that it fairly begs for explanation. Its maker, a young man, believes that his image reflects his drive for perfection and here he finds perfection in symmetry. The son of a "total" perfectionist father, he is a perfectionist himself. In his life he attempts to prove to himself that he has control over people and things, and these range from an innocuous confidence in being able to lose weight whenever he wishes or study hard whenever he decides, to unwelcome attempts to run his schoolmates' lives. With so pure, perhaps relentless, a pursuit of control, he serves as an ideal example of this style, and I shall discuss him more fully at the end of the chapter.

Urbania, although less decorative and more plausibly projected into three-dimensional space, comes quite close to *Framed Flowers* in its rigid organization. Its feeling tone is, however, strident, antiutopian, and oppositional. Done by a young man majoring in biochemistry and minoring in computer science, it was based on the *Village* picture and chosen because there was a "lot going on in the picture that I could manipulate". He worked by cutting elements from the original picture and pasting them onto a blank frame of exactly the same size—but in a more orderly way. (He compared his process to the Orwellian one from *1984* in which people were edited from pictures after they had been gotten rid of.) Nevertheless, he did not see his process as planful; he "played it by ear", "just going along and manipulating things not in any particular direction". (In this he may have been forestalling any eventual disappointment with his image; as it was, he did tell us that he was satisfied, there being "no serious errors" in it.) Having said that, however, he also made clear that he was "in the business of making tract houses", and went on to say that although he had grown up in a tract community, his early experience had nothing to do with his present image. We are inclined to see his image as a metaphor for his covert opposition to his father—covert because although "he" himself stands out in the picture as a red house in a drab field, he also remains hidden—but this is only a guess, and we suspect that as with other issues he might have addressed this one had we asked. As it is, approval from a person in authority is something he sought even while doing his image, as when he would bring the experimenter into the process by suggesting that "they" do this or that together.

Working meticulously, he was intent on making the houses look photorealistic; this included the chimney pipes which reminded him of his work pipes and hoses in biochemistry. He liked the big house because "it looks like something growing up and sprouting", and balanced it with the little red house on the left.

He is the son of a very analytical and unemotional psychologist father who has a strong sense of protocol, such as which relatives to say hello to first, and of a compulsive cleaner of a mother; he sees himself as similar to his father and agrees with him in most things, but is also like his mother in liking to have things clean and meticulous. To this day she calls him in his dorm room to find out if he has made his bed. He describes his relationship to his parents as very good, and among his interests describes several that might suggest a respect for authority and religion in spite of having been raised as an atheist: Gregorian chants, Latin Mass, medieval texts, and calligraphy. In fact one of his avocational goals is to become a better calligrapher, something that suggests a search for perfection in a realm with clear rules; consistent with this, he is quite self-critical and easily chastises himself for past mistakes. Although he is in a romantic relationship now, he and his girl friend both put their career interests first and know that they will be parted in their pursuits of their career goals.

The painter of **Suburbia**, also a young man in his early twenties, also began with the *Village* picture and also chose it because he thought it would be the most interesting to manipulate. He, too, worked very rhythmically and repetitively to multiply the houses and their landscaping, and did keep a part of the image uninterpretable; in his case the obscure element was the street sign which was in a foreign language (which remained undisclosed to us). Like the maker of *Urbania*, he worked painstakingly and made sure his houses had windows; but unlike him, he made them large and mirrorlike, and saw the process not as one of making tract houses but remodeling old ones. When asked if the image had a meaning, he too was cryptic and self-contradictory; he remarked, "development all the way. Not really."

The son of an electronic technician father and an accountant mother, he described his father as authoritarian and remembered growing up with him as confusing: the father was very demanding, but "you never knew what he wanted, he wouldn't express it, he would only express what he didn't like." In fact his father's expectations were never clear: they were that he get good grades, be respectful, and not get into trouble— emphasizing, it would seem, correctness and the observance of rules rather than any particular substance. The son did miss having clearer guidelines, and we suspect that he is as highly self-critical as he is because the goals presented to him were as unattainable as they were vague.

Wishing he could see himself as different from his father, as he did when he was young, he now realizes that he is as fanatical about cleanliness as his dad: "I have this urge to clean and have it clean like he considers clean". His mother had never hugged him or kissed him when he was younger, and he felt she was cold, but she has become more supportive and caring and he now makes an effort to be more physical by hugging and kissing her. To this image of coldness and unattainable standards we must add the parents' conditional love, which he felt would be retracted whenever they were displeased; though he is fairly easygoing now, he, too, used to be conditional in his romantic relationships. He described love as "just as sense of comfort inside of you about that other person, an easygoing and relaxed attitude"; he has a relationship with a man which had started in high school, and has had other, briefer ones as well.

Our impression is that in their images both young men are creating representations of something vague they had always been expected to attain but, thanks to its vagueness, could not; order and orderliness seem the best metaphors for this unattainable thing.

The young woman who painted **Spectrum** creates a more focused metaphor for her family life. She describes her image as showing "chaos on the outside and it's whole in the middle", and describes its meaning as "it's kind of like me, exploding all over the place. I identify with it ... well, I wish I could identify with it more: the lines and circles are so definite." Proceeding from four separate starts on two different images, she worked carefully but tentatively, and was frustrated easily and found circles particularly difficult to make.

She gives us a very clear clue to the meaning of her metaphor. She recalls playing in the garden as a small child while her father would draw and paint her; over time, however, his painterly interests shifted from representational work to more abstract work, and eventually to drawing mandalas; he also switched to pharmacy. One can understand if she saw this as a withdrawal on his part and found it painful, and it makes sense to view the present image as her attempt to bridge the gap.

It seems all the more plausible when we look at the father's development over the years. Married to an elementary school teacher, he always fought with his wife; family life was volatile, the mother would "mindlessly yell", and the family would divide into alliances (which easily changed). The young woman withdrew into her room and became a loner, humorless and easily offended. Her mother still "blocks her out" and seems uninterested in her, but at least the parents get along better. Above all, the father has become a Buddhist monk and controls his anger through meditation. Her image's chaos outside the circle and the hoped for order within, the choice of a mandala as the symbol of order—the connections to the family's chaos, to the loss of paternal attention, and to the father's newfound self-control, are only too clear.

I might add, about her present relationships, that although she has just entered into one—she is a freshman—she finds it easier to be friends than lovers. Sex is not all that important, it can be misused as a way of manipulating a partner, and one needs to be concerned that the partner be clean.

Religion, recently found rather than inculcated early on, plays a role in the work and psychological dynamics of the man—an art and biology major in his early thirties—who created *The Persistence of Beauty*. He had worked hard and assiduously at his image, meticulously and often under high magnification, at first subdividing it into facets like those of stained glass, which he also makes, then—for a full hour—blurring everything except the lily and one of the roses in order to "cover his tracks". He felt he was done "when I made the final connection between the process and the statement." As mistrustful as he says he is of the destructiveness of analytical thinking, he could only talk about the image in an analytical and stilted way: its meaning is that "the effects of intellectualization or analyzing have been a separation of society from natural beauty around us."

In his early thirties, he is a very thoughtful individual who has worked hard to glean the best of his parents' and grandparents' traits. His parents, although recently divorced, were together throughout his growing up, and he was close to his grandparents on both sides. Refined in his tastes, he has been intellectually and spiritually oriented since embracing Christian teaching and being mentored by a Benedictine monk, and now draws daily on Taoist philosophy to help guide his life. Unlike the other subjects, he describes his parents with balance and appropriate distance, noting their negative as well as their positive qualities. His father is rather overbearing and aggressive—he had been "overly ardent" in his physical discipline—and our painter works to maintain a distance from him; the father would like him to be a Casanova, and to hold the view that the universe is meaningless, but the son instead seeks spiritual meaning and is inhibited in his romantic relationships, having had only two and both without sex.

One has the sense of this young man as very attentive to his elders and their values, and carefully choosing among them—all the more so as he needed to find a direction for his life opposed to that of his father. We believe that he has been helped in this by his identification with his mother in certain qualities he values: patience, perceptiveness of subtleties, and sharing a taste for finer things such as good design and cohesiveness. There is almost a willful love of beauty in him, a conviction that beauty persists and will win out because it is present in the smallest things. This kind of willful control has a precedent in his dealings with anger. Normally feeling and expressing it freely—perhaps too freely, he says—he has been learning to walk away from provocations instead of meeting them head-on; earlier, he had struck a man in the face who had tried to silence his piano playing. I am inclined to think that precisely because the belief in the persistence of beauty is a conviction, beauty has to be imposed on the original image in the form of an ordered scheme; to trust in its natural, immanent presence seems more than he can do.

The young man who created **Waterfall** was much less thoughtful and worked without a plan or program, but in several respects his mode of working resembled the painter of *Persistence*: he worked carefully, smudged a lot to join his assembled image, and was pleased with his straight lines. After he had combined the two original landscapes into one, he drew the sun and its rays, and having done that felt that the image was finally coming together. He then conceived of the waterfall, drew it very carefully, and eventually colored in the little house on the right. He found it easy to express both happiness and frustration, but not to comment on the meaning of what he was doing: the image "had no meaning" except that he likes imaginary places.

In his later interview he was friendly but often ill at ease with the personal questions and evasive in a polite way—as for example by turning the more intimate questions into impersonal, general ones. The middle child of three, he finds his parents happily married, both working. He identifies with his father more than he realizes: "he's kind of simple-natured like myself ... just does what he does and he doesn't really do much besides what he does". We believe, as he explains this, that he connects his mode of being with his mode of working: "and that's kind of the way I am, like it's hard for me to break from certain routines that I get used to, so I mean I *do*, but usually once someone drags me along"—reflecting, it seems, the careful kind of graphic work he does as an art student as well as the precise work here. When he adds, "we just like to make an effort to be happy all the time", he suggests a willful effort, somewhat like the mechanically imposed brilliant sun in his image. His mother is artistic, which is where he says he got his art and music, and has certain unspecified compulsions, which he says he has, too.

Quite passive, he was happy that the young woman with whom he is involved now had initiated their meeting, and is frustrated in the relationship only when he feels that he is giving her more attention than she gives him. We find out that they are best friends, but we do not learn anything about his feelings or passions. And when we ask him about his level of self-acceptance, he answers with a revealing tautology: "I live my life by the way that I want to, and I basically pretty much follow my own rules, and because of that I have no reason to not accept who I am because who I am is what I have made myself to be." This suggests a certain unwillingness to plumb his own feelings; he has adopted a structure for what he should feel and how he should be. This kind of willfulness helps us understand, I think, at least his imposition of the artificial sun and the lack of spontaneous, coherent meaning.

Wish You Were Here, as a title, suggests a picture postcard, and it is indeed as such that it was meant. The young woman who created it is an art major, and she chose the Village picture as her subject because it reminded her of the trip to Europe that she was about to take and of the hopes for a more ideal life there that she entertained. She intended from the start to import flowers from the still life to make a border, and copied, cut, rotated and pasted the flowers repeatedly while cleaning up the edges of her work meticulously. She was aware of how many flowers of each kind she had used and thought carefully about the compositional and numerical balance of the border.

An only child, she was raised by her parents, who have been together for 27 years. She describes them—and their relation, as well as the family life—in loving terms, and is best friends with her mother. Because she refused to go along with the crowd—and because, we think, her tie to her mother was stronger than the tie to her peers—she felt left out and picked on by other children. She describes two romantic relationships in which she had been mistreated, one of which is still ongoing, and another current one with a man who is "like my dad or brother and sister". Unsure of what to make of this, we suspect from her answer to the question about the importance of sex that the relationship is altogether platonic; "sex, oooh: that's not a big factor; I am willing to wait."

To steer the conversation to safer topics she resorts to giddiness and silliness, and to avoid a deeper connection with her own thoughts and feelings she resorts to clichés; she makes many sarcastic or joking remarks and enjoys making the interviewer laugh. She explains that her mother has a cliché for everything and that she got that from her mother in turn, which suggests to her that it will carry on from generation to generation. One of her own clichés is that she is a Pisces, easily swimming in both directions, which she can use to explain any contradiction she does not wish to think further about. She is unclear, for example, about whether she is decisive or not: on the one hand she does not get passionately committed to things—which explains her present unsureness of direction—while on the other once she has figured out what to do, "you can't shake it loose". Perhaps both statements are right: unsure of an inner direction, she will hold on firmly to a direction once adopted. In any case she is clear in describing herself as meticulous and tidy, more so than her mother. Of these various defenses against her inner world, in her image we see the pollyannish gloss, and the tidiness, most clearly.

Tidiness and strong identification with an older figure, but not the pollyannish gloss, are present in the woman who created **Garden of Eden**. Working without a plan, she spent a lot of time testing out the electronic tools—the filters and the many ways of transforming hues, color balances, and saturations—and made two starts on her image, both of which she saved and eventually incorporated into each other. She described her process as "anal" and then laughed, self-consciously, for having said so. She noticed that she had spent a lot of time making very few changes and at the last minute labeled the fruit as his and hers and entitled the image the Garden of Eden.

Unlike the author of *Wish You were Here*, she is and has been distant from her mother and father and they seem to have been distant from each other—so much so that she used to wonder when it was that they did speak to each other. Although she did have "yelling fights" with them, she gives us a picture of her family life as essentially isolating. She recalls trying to engage with her mother, who was always reading the newspaper, and finding that the mother would not put the paper down. She was no closer to her sister, or her best friend, with both of whom her relations were highly competitive and envious. Nevertheless, she spoke with genuine warmth—with love and affection—about an older neighbor who lived next door, but whom she never saw again after moving to California in the 6th grade, and whose death she only learned about from a returned Christmas card.

She has come to resemble her mother in her distance from herself: "my friends and boyfriends say that I never talk about myself, that

I don't say what I am thinking, feeling or doing, or what my plans are". In a way, she has not had any really personal relationships and has neither been in love nor known what love in a relationship really is. One can, then, see an inhibition in most of her emotional functioning, which is perhaps even stronger than that of the rest of the group, and a perfectionism that protects her from facing her inner world.

In *My Mother's Garden* (Fig. 61) the presence of perfectionism is as palpable as it is in the life of the artist. She knew at all times that she was working toward some form of perfection, and though she found the pressure toward perfection inescapable, she also found it quite normal: that is how she does everything. She tried not to have a plan while working, but did confess later that one idea governed her from the start: to get rid of the roses. She did so, slowly and methodically, and distorted the lily somewhat and multiplied the white flowers until there were enough of them.

Her self-described perfectionism constitutes in many ways a full explanation of her goals and mode of working, but there are some details in her relation to flowers, particularly roses, and some complexities in her relationship with her mother and father, that explain the need for perfection itself. I shall reserve this for detailed treatment at the end of the chapter.

The artist who created **Mine** chose the still life because she "wanted to work with each thing separately and make a whole picture". Picking her colors carefully, often from the picture itself, and counting petals to make sure alternating colors would come out even, she worked precisely at creating a decorative scheme, adding a happy and a sad face, and eliminating the pink lily. Trying the title "Happy-Sad" at first, she settled on "Mine". She saw the picture as related to her life because it is precise, and because she is a perfectionist who has done things precisely since she was in first grade, keeping things in what she calls "rainbow order". She knew she had a visceral revulsion to the color pink, although she used to like it until she was ten years old. We only find out some of the meanings of the word "mine" in the later interview.

A young woman of 18, she speaks at length about her family structure. She grew up the daughter of a young couple who had met in college and who separated when she was two and a half; she then alternated between the parents until the mother remarried, when she chose to live with her father, and when the father remarried in turn, with the new couple. She is close to her father but visits her mother during the summers. Adults have always been important to her—she would play with the "aunts" and "uncles" of her parents' early, group household years, rather than with children—and this was a source of pleasure as well as ambivalence: she feels that she had received too much unconditional praise and has not learned who she "really is". We were as struck by her thoroughness in orienting the interviewer to her family's history as by its omission of significant emotional material. There are two exceptions. One is that she hints at events that we would imagine to be distressing to her, such as the sudden revulsion to pink which she vaguely connects to her stepmother's family; the other is that she recognizes the importance of the loss of her stepmother's family following her father's second separation. She says she will miss the family—particularly the grandfather—whom, like all her extended relatives, she considers "mine". She is also glad that, unlike her mother who spent all the money she had inherited from her father, she still has her inheritance in trust: "but mine I still have".

Her parents' goals for her were unclear—her mother was removed and irresponsible in any case—but her stepmother's goals were "high and nothing was good enough". Without being able to say what she wanted, the stepmother simply criticized everything and tried to make up for the way other adults had spoiled her by telling her everything that she did wrong. Her own goals are to find a man who would make a good father and raise "healthy, beautiful children"; she is breaking away from a three-year relationship that had started in high school and is beginning to see someone else, but she sees no point in a committed relationship at present. She would like to find sex important, but her last experience has been negative. She does, in any case, like romantic novels: "I love things that have happy endings". In our view, the main issue that animates her is the possession of a family, and the dominant style is both perfectionistic and pollyannish—a style which, put more technically, relies on manic denial. The main issue is her own, but the style is shared with most of the other participants.

Like the creator of Mine, the maker of **Mieru** chose to work with the still life and worked meticulously, often adding single pixels under high magnification. She said she loves flowers and the picture had many more bright colors than the others; approaching it, she did not want to change it or "ruin" it, but did want to alter it enough so that it would be "unnatural" and "different", while remaining like a "real picture". At one point she was also clear that she wanted to get rid of the pink in the picture, because—like the creator of Mine—she does not like pink. (We now have three women painters who confess to that aversion—and who have all selected this flower arrangement to work on—and cannot but suspect a pattern; but only the painter of My Mother's Garden, who will be presented in detail, was able to tell us why.) Beyond that she said she had no plan, and would look to see what she could find in the image. Careful of imposing on the experimenter, she invited her to take a break from writing whenever she needed it and, concerned about the time, she hoped she wasn't "being too detailed". One might say about her that she is genuinely timid, albeit in a most considerate way.

Raised by her mother and her stepfather from the age of three, she describes her stepfather, a naval officer, as domineering, very demanding, and very strict—and yet as having no particular goals for her; she had a combative relation to him, arguing with him for years because he always had to be right. Her mother was subservient to him but loving nevertheless, and has a very warm and caring relationship with her daughter. All in all our painter is more like him than like her—she too is set in her ways and opinionated, finding it hard to look at both sides of an issue. She can also feel strong anger and has been known to kick walls, hard enough to break a toe. In an identity crisis now—having just entered college—she does not know what she wants to do. In high school she tried to revive the Christianity that she had been raised in, but hearing from someone that "all Buddhists were going to hell", she decided it was not for her.

Her defenses, we observe, are not altogether pollyannish; she is complex enough to find that romantic movies and soap operas belittle life, and it is possibly this complexity that allows for the intrusion of the bulging eye into an otherwise decorative picture, just as anger is allowed to intrude into her life. She explains that the word *Mieru* is Japanese for "to see", but we never do find out who is looking at whom, nor why. But insofar as there are polyannish defenses at work, they seem connected with a fear of death that she first experienced after the death of an uncle; she would have dreams of earthquakes and the ground cracking, until every member of her family had disappeared.

THE PSYCHOLOGICAL DYNAMICS OF THIS CLUSTER

In one sense our painters have given us a straightforward picture of their need for formality: they all describe themselves as meticulous, tidy, precise, or perfectionistic, and with one exception (*Waterfall*), self-critical. They have a clear model for this in their parents, one or both of whom were in technical, asocial occupations. At a deeper level, they suggest the conditions under which the models were accepted: they all grew up in intact nuclear families or families with a constant stepparent for most of their childhood, and many of them felt close to at least one parent if not both. Those whose parents were emotionally distant found that the parents nevertheless presented a united front, or found other parental figures to identify with. *All the painters, in short, grew up in conditions favoring the acceptance of parental or adult standards, but the standards they were asked to accept might be quite vague*, as in the expectation that they be respectful; invariably, what the young people identified with would reflect a process without an end-product: perfectionism.

At a yet deeper level, I believe that the perfectionism serves as a defense: to distance them from their inner world. This might result in their not knowing what they thought or felt, or in an inhibition of affection or sexuality, or in a pollyannish view of the world. (And it might account for the "banality" seen in their images when they were rated for the purposes of the cluster analysis.) Only in one respect is the defense permeable, and that is that the painters are easily angered and defend against the anger consciously, in a form that is once again technically manic. Most of them have also looked for adult controls in religion— a religion which they discovered late rather than being raised in it.

Finally, I am in a position to comment on the quality of hiding, and inviting discovery, that could be seen in some specific symbols. Of course, one may think of *any* order that is imposed on the world rather than immanent as suggesting hiding, but there are symbols here which say so specifically: silvered windows, missing flowers, faces and eyes peering out of flowers. They appear to symbolize the barriers our artists put up against self-knowledge. Being aware of it as an issue (as the painter of *Garden of Eden* was when she said, "my friends ... say that I never talk about myself, that I don't say what I am thinking, feeling or doing"), they have reason to grapple with it now.

Now we can look at two individuals in more detail; they each illustrate a particular quality of the drive for perfection that tells us why it should be so unrelenting. In the first painter it is a trauma which exacerbated and confirmed a style which was already being formed by identification with his father, while in the second it is the elusiveness of the perfectionist's goals.

FRAMED FLOWERS

Throughout his work on his image, Roger, as I shall call him, was aware that his approach reflected his drive for perfection. He was aware, too, of a wish to work on something no one had done before.

Figure 60. Framed Flowers

Although two-dimensional images were not as comfortable for him as working in clay or constructing something practical might have been, his frustration was tolerable and he was able to enlist the tester's help with the most intractable technical problems. He would go back and forth between the original image and a blank slate, copying flowers and pasting them into his concentric frames until he was content.

Roger is well aware that his striving for perfection and need for order are evident in other activities as well. When we asked him to give us an example, he thought of the project he has been engaged in for six months of taping CDs. "I am very critical about getting the right kind of tape, ... getting the recording level right, and I even started making tape covers on my roommate's computer just to kill time, but at the same time I feel sort of obsessed with it in a way." Striving for perfection and reaching it are not one and the same thing, however, and he is aware that he often falls short—he is critical of his writing, for example ("I was in the habit of writing papers the night before and I am never going to get perfection if I do that"), and of his study habits ("I just don't feel I know the right method to study"). He likes to prove to himself that he is in control: disappointed in a swimming coach who did not adequately focus on him to help him become better, he swam on for himself: "It's like just proving to myself that I can go and just do it … . I have good will power and I can commit myself to something, like one summer I decided I was overweight so I tried this diet and lost some weight and I felt a lot better, then I started to get sick of it and just ended it. But it gives me a new thinking about how to eat."

He admires his father, a dentist, who always works for perfection. "He's a total perfectionist, and I think that part of that has rubbed off on me." He was not pushed into it, he says, it has simply rubbed off: "I like that side of him because it sort of pushes me to perfection in a lot of cases." He has, indeed, considered dentistry as a career and even thought of working with his father. Perfectionism seems to be the single quality with which he identifies; in other respects, he feels different. Where his father was a model student, the son, for example, has to struggle to stay in college, and this is on the contrary a point of resemblance to his mother. She is both emotional and outgoing, very exciting as well as very mellow at times, and the emotional side at least is something he has, too. Although he says that he resembles his mother in lots of ways, he is hard put to name any others, and his own emotionality is not without its mysteries and complexities.

He believes that he is emotionally expressive with people, sometimes so much so that it scares a lot of people away. He says that he likes to meet people, but it is also clear that he tends to alienate them by being critical and controlling; one wonders if what he sees as his emotional openness is not in fact a readiness to criticize. He is, in fact, more isolated than not. As a child, he had a hard time fitting in; he was picked on by other kids until he started taking karate in eighth grade, and after that he wasn't picked on any more, but he still did not have any intimate friends. As he sees it, he has had friends who were best friends but he could not rely on them; he could never find anyone as strong as he. "I hang around a person for a certain amount of time and usually I find that they are just not for me." The friends he has right now are more like "satellites"—a term which he leaves undefined—and this seems to throw him back on his identification with his parents. "I would say that my best friends are probably my parents."

The problem with making and keeping friends seems ultimately to be one of control and criticism. In high school, "I was alive, awake, and I realized finally they weren't as awake as I thought they were. I knew they weren't awake but ... since there were so many of them, trapped, it sort of closed in on me. I got the wacky idea to start the club called The Awareness Club ... . That idea lasted for three days, ... L.A. sort of threw me down and snuffed me out like a cigarette butt ... . I gave up on them, sort of closed up." He is not without humor as he recounts this, but seems not to see how deep was his need to control others' lives even when he could think it was for their own good.

The roots of perfectionism and control may be many, such as an identification with a perfectionist father, but in Roger's life we can see one single event that would have exacerbated any earlier and slower process of identification: the death of a beloved grandfather in a plane crash when he was in second grade. He remembers coming home from school with everyone crying and his uncle going nuts. "I think it was because in our family he was sort of like the person in control, he was controlling not only his three children and their families but also his two sisters and their families, and his mother, sort of like the Godfather of the family." As a result of the death the extended family split apart. His own memory of his childhood became hazy from this moment on, and he felt that he then grew up very quickly. "It wasn't something that I felt I needed to do. It just happened, you know; it ... definitely changed me."

The fear of loss of control could not but work hand in glove with the perfection he admired in his father. It is almost as if there were no other way his character could have been formed. One can hardly imagine a more fitting metaphor for wishing to reimpose control than a perfectly organized, repetitive, box-within-box arrangement of flowers.

MY MOTHER'S GARDEN

Daphne is no less a perfectionist, but her formation was somewhat different and both her image and her life seem to have their feet more firmly planted in the ground. Like Roger she makes clear that parents are the source of the perfectionist's standards, but more clearly than he, she tells us that the standards are always unattainable.

Like the artist who created *Mine*, she "avoided thinking about a plan; ... I didn't want to have any expectations because I didn't want to feel let down about it, if I didn't live up to what I wanted to do." At the end, however, she did confess that the work was "a process toward some kind of perfection, which is hard to do when you don't have some ideal in mind. All you know is you have to be perfect. Somehow you have to attain a goal." This attempt at self-protection against criticism was joined by a plan for the image's content: she knew from the start that she wanted to get rid of the roses.

She had selected the flower image to work on because she was drawn to the bright colors, but they were too bright and she wanted to mute them. She began working on the lily, under high magnification, building up transparent layers of color over it, but discovering the filters suddenly, she decided that she preferred distorting the flowers to coloring them, erased her earlier work, and started over. Her working time was spent "returning to things over and over again, to see what she could do to them," very much as in all her other activities, which include her academic papers and her photography work, where she keeps "returning to things until I'm absolutely satisfied with them." She worked slowly and methodically, humming as she worked, and betrayed a bit of tension as she bit her nail cuticles.

When she was done she entitled the work *My Mother's Garden*, and explained that her mother loved flowers and flower arrangements and that this was in some sense an ode to her. But the term "ode" was as ambivalent as her relationship to her mother. Because her mother dislikes unconventional things, Daphne was going to distort the flowers and make the image unconventional. Having finished, however, she realized that for the amount of time she had spent working she had made the changes very subtle indeed, and that she had not opposed her mother much at all. "It's [after all] a lot like the way I've seen my mother do things, which is funny, because I was trying to do something opposite to the way she works." So an ode to the garden became simply the garden itself.

Her attempt to get rid of the roses was also part of the wish to make the image unconventional, but she soon discovered a deeper meaning.

Figure 61. My Mother's Garden

At first claiming that roses were unimaginative and traditional, because everyone gave them, she told us shortly after finishing that they reminded her of a childhood incident. "I realized in thinking about it that it was my best friend's from high school favorite flower. They always had them all over the house, ... especially pink flowers. I had a falling out with her ... . Her stepfather molested me. And four other friends that we know about. She and her mother did not believe me; I was accused of having a crush on him. Then last year a friend of mine went into counselling and it came out through the child protection agency. He's not being prosecuted because of the statute of limitations."

This memory, then, hangs over her like a dark cloud. All of the young women have been affected by it in some way—some distrusting men and others, like Daphne, distrusting women—and she feels that the incident cannot be closed. Because of the statute of limitations, "it's totally unresolvable; it's not an option."

She is, then, bound both to her mother and to this memory. Her father—an emotionally distant corporate comptroller who communicates with Daphne only through the metaphor of money—is nevertheless honest and intelligent, and a man of integrity who is almost predictable. The word "almost" makes sense when contrasted with the character of the mother—who is also in finance—which is "completely unpredictable; you never know what kind of mood she is going to be in or how quickly her mood is going to change." She goes on right away to say that her mother always attempted to control her: "Our problem is that we both wanted to be in charge of me. If she told me to sit down, I would stand up." Added to this constant opposition is the sense that the mother is irrational, does not listen to people, and glories in making people cry.

Yet Daphne cannot reject this altogether because she is too much like her: she, too, is moody and will fly off the handle if someone "breathes wrong and it upsets me," and moreover, like her mother, she is bossy, condescending, and demanding with men. She understands her mother only too well: her own father had been a very controlling person, one who could not tolerate his daughter growing up and wanted to keep her a child; Daphne remembers him well, because he attempted to impose the same control on her. (The image of control harking back to the grandparental generation is, curiously, reminiscent of Roger's history.) If she identifies more strongly than she would like with the mother's anger and opposition, she at least takes comfort in being able to control them by living up to her idealized father's expectations: "My biggest fear is losing my father's respect. I respect him so much. I love him so much. I don't want him to stop loving me."

One might say that Daphne is a perfectionist in spite of herself—that, in trying to oppose the mother's carping she imposes too much of the father's control, and finds it hard to move away from either. The tie that binds her to her parents may well speak for the other perfectionists here, too; in any case, she puts it succinctly when she says, "I think it doesn't matter what your friends say or what your boyfriend says, as far as I am concerned ... it comes down to what your immediate family says. And I think that's who you are always trying to please throughout your life. You're trying to live up to them, and what they expect of you, and when you don't get your encouragment, I think you try harder and harder on your own to achieve something."

CHAPTER 8

Sixth Cluster

Consistent Style and the Need to Integrate

On the surface the four images constituting this small cluster do not look alike.[1] *Enchanted Sicily* is quite closely based on the photograph that served as its starting point and retains its natural space and recognizable objects; it seems to avoid all suggestion of stylized vision. *Fruit Tree* and *Colors* preserve much of the shape and rhythms of the persimmon leaf picture, while giving the surface a stylish consistency. *Temple Cluster*, on the other hand, transforms its flat, arid model into a bare suggestion of a lush, deep landscape with a flowing river. Granted, they are all three-dimensional to some degree, but that is not the quality our cluster analysis says they share.

What they do share is the quality we had judged from the manner in which they had been made: the process was flowing rather than saccadic, the image was moving rather than static and diffuse rather than sharp, the effect of the whole sparse rather than dense, and the preferred manipulations hands-on rather than mechanical. And the

---

[1] The cluster consists of five images in fact, and meets the minimum size requirement for a solution based on five factors, as ours was. The fifth subject's image is as close to the characteristics of cluster 4 as to this one, however; this ambiguity is best resolved by leaving him out of the discussion.

If we had opted for the minimum to be larger, forcing these five images into one of the other clusters, they would have all been assigned to cluster 3—another cluster composed mostly of artists. That one was characterized as bold in its approach and flowing in its process, underscoring the Flowing dimension as the one they all have in common. It seemed more meaningful, however, to attend to what sets these five artists apart from the others; these create formal images, while the others made loose, gestural ones. We believe that our choice was right in retrospect—except, as we say, for the marginal fifth subject.

making of the image showed an emphasis on form and on integrating the form with the original image.

If we look at the images again, we can now see the emphasis on form: they are all internally consistent in some way, either gestural or compositional, unified in a way that suggests consistency of purpose. And yes, they take care to transform the original image by a hands-on application of a consistent vision—rather than, for example, by cutting and reassembling it, pasting projections onto it, or seeing it through a succession of mechanical filters. In this way, they become highly aesthetic, and while they are not the only images in our study to become aesthetic, they are the only ones to strive for form less from an accumulation of gestures than through a consistent vision.

Perhaps not coincidentally, all of the subjects are artists.[2] They have in fact achieved or at least practiced an individual style and, although the work on the computer was new to them, they approached it with the expectation of finding a style appropriate to the new medium. The psychological question changes emphasis, then: rather than asking what they are trying to express, we need to ask what they are trying to unify, and why they need to unify at all. Since there are only four subjects, we can discuss them all as individuals, two briefly and two at length, and allow their shared characteristics to emerge at the end.

THE PSYCHOLOGICAL PROCESS

The young man who created **Enchanted Sicily** prepared himself carefully and worked meticulously: knowing that he would try to make his work look like a painting, he first tried various filters, rejected them all as mechanical, and only retained a bit of the granularity produced by the Add Noise filter. With this as a ground, he spent time preparing a palette of colors consistent with his purpose. It was clear to him that, as he put it later, "it was an enchanted site for me, and it speaks of a timeless quality of place that all artists have gone to see ... a sense of place that speaks of a feeling of nature speaking to the painter." Seeing it for the first time, he said to himself, "I see trails in this painting, so I imagined a road that would lead down the hill, so as to reach this plane ... gradually into this shrubbery."

He translated his understanding of the photograph's challenge into the wish to interconnect all aspects of the image ("I wanted to dramatize, to create more of a feeling that everything was connected"). So he

[2] As was the fifth subject.

Figure 62. Enchanted Sicily

Figure 63. Colors

tied the foreground to the background by means of the road, evened out the quality of light by putting dark shrubbery into the hillside and shadows into the foreground and, above all, drew myriad light blue dots in the trees and yellow ones in the hills. "These are the spirits of the trees in nature calling forth the artist to paint. It could be these little spirits in nature, spirits of inspiration, or tiny little muses calling from the leaves of the trees ... ." Attentive to formal concerns, he clarified the bottom center by giving firm stems to the bushes; and aware of his wish to transform a mere scene into a painting, he gave the sky a rough, brush-like treatment. He knew he was done when he could squint his eyes and "see that these things bleed into one another to create a lot of, not a feeling of separateness, but a feeling that it's related or connected, that there is a feeling of cohesiveness about it."

His transformation are, indeed, gentle and his pace was comparably slow and deliberate. He achieved the integration he sought not by imposing a unique handwriting vigorously, but by searching for a kind of immanent unity within the scene and showing us his own connection with it. He was aware of the particular appeal of this picture: it reminded him of the dry landscape and the relentless sun of the desert in his native Southern California, and of the Greek myths that he connects with Sicily. He was aware, also, of the meaning of the path he drew on the far hillside: it stood, among others, for his wish to be connected with the tradition of painting. He had in mind in particular the masterly integrations of the landscapes of Cézanne and Corot.

And he revealed still deeper connections in his interview. A Native American, he was made aware early of the close connection of man with nature; the son of a strong, even-tempered father, he has early memories of sleeping on his lap and feeling his big hands, strong as steel. His mother, a giving woman and superb cook (but also a subtly controlling woman, he says) was a self-taught pastel artist who inspired him when he was small. Now in his mid-twenties, he lives with his two older brothers in their close-knit family when he is not in school. He is in no hurry to leave, but accepts that it will happen in its time; his oldest brother is about to take the step. Perhaps because he is still attached to his parental home, he is not yet experienced sexually, but in this he is following the example of his father, who waited until he had found the right woman when he was in his late thirties and then remained faithful to her. Interconnectedness is everywhere in his life, then: with nature, between parents and children, and between siblings. It is the leitmotif of his life, and in a way it is sufficient for understanding his art, but it does raise a question: is the wish heightened in any way? I suggest that it may well be exacerbated by the tension between his idealization of women and his hesitant, inhibited, approach to them.

The young woman who painted **Colors** achieved an integration of a different kind. As someone who has "done art all her life" and whose mother, brother, and two uncles are all artistic, she would seek expressive consistency as a matter of habit; but her way of seeking it is quite unplanned and her intentions in general are barely formulated. Starting with the picture of persimmon leaves, she finds it too strongly composed and too unambiguous, and thinks that it needs "fuzzing up" to make it easier to build on; to do this, she tries a number of filters. They seem to produce the wrong effect, so she rejects them all and begins to work by hand on the background; while saying "I don't know what I am doing; just playing," she seems on the evidence to have a reasonably clear intention: to give the background more color and a texture of its own.

She works on it entirely by hand with colors she picks beforehand and stores for use. Working back and forth between background and leaves, she also brightens the leaves as much as possible; she works loosely, quickly and with vigorous gestures. At one point she remarks, "everything is on the surface, there is no depth; I want to punch holes in it". She seems on the one hand closely aware of form but on the other unsure of what form she wants to strive for. Whatever her balance of intention and gesture, shortly before finishing she has a very colorful but utterly turbulent image before her. Then, almost as an afterthought, she picks up the Pencil and draws a few lines within the leaves and adds sketchy outlines to their edges, and is done. The end result seems unified and aesthetic, loose yet harnessed.

Afterwards she is happy with the lines she has added; although she always uses a lot of color in her paintings, she needed these lines to give the picture focus. Asked if the picture relates to her life in any way, she implies at first that it does not because "it's kind of haphazard", and then changes her mind: "I guess you could turn it around and say it's like my life. I didn't have any plans, it just happened, and that is how I go sometimes—if something looks right, I'll do it." In the personal interview that follows she gives us enough information to agree with her—in essence—and to add something of our own.

The daughter of divorced parents, she has a real father whom she would not choose for a friend, so conservative and authoritarian is he, and a step-father who is reserved, tall, and imposing—and frightening. On the other hand her mother is open, liberal, friendly and outgoing, and a very close friend; she is the sort of person to whom people open up in supermarkets. Our painter is much more like her and identifies with her,

Figure 64. Fruit Tree

and is close enough and trusting enough to show her her art work. Although she has not had either a romantic or a sexual relationship yet, she expects to do so; in the meantime she has resolved to avoid the mistake her mother had made in marrying someone she did not know very well. In the interview she is alternately giddy and light, and somewhat depressed; she is certainly shy. When we ask if she is emotionally expressive, she says that she does not always know her emotions; she does her expressing with her art work. When we ask if she is aggressive or assertive, the answer is again negative, but then she tells us that her thoughts are quite violent; perhaps the memories of the father who brought home rabbit tails that he had just shot off, or of her ill-tempered step-father, are implicated here.

Our impression is that the poles of her being are somewhat far apart, and that this distance is reflected in her picture. She would like to be both expressive and assertive, as is her mother, and as she expects to become later, but in the meantime, she realizes this only in her art. Sometimes she does so to excess; but here, toward the end of the work, she realized that she had to impose a kind of masculine control and chose black lines to do it (see the meaning of lines and colors in the work of the subject who made *Temple Cluster*). A picture which was turbulent at first then attains some restraint. It may not reflect a conscious wish for connectedness or integration, as in the painter of *Enchanted Sicily*, but it seems to parallel an effort after balance in her own life. Like his, her art is produced under the added tension of needs unsatisfied in life.

However brief this discussion, it suggests a formulation: *these subjects use style to unify their psychological world.* Style in these two individuals is more than a mere gestural progression formed of habit; it soon reveals itself as purposeful and symbolic, designed to satisfy a wish for integration. Does it serve the same purpose in the other two subjects? They themselves make clear to us that it does.

FRUIT TREE

An undeniable self-assurance marks the approach of the woman who came to call her picture *Fruit Tree*. "Natasha" prepares several colors for future use, both from the color picker and from the image, and saves them. They include an olive green, a khaki yellow, the persimmon color, and a green brown; she will add others later as needed. She says that she is trying to proceed as if she were doing a painting and preparing a palette. She had chosen the *Leaves* picture to work on because it was already reasonably flat and easier to integrate, as if it were already a canvas.

With her first touch, she doubles the outline of one of the leaves with the olive green, and begins to paint a face. We come to understand the purpose of the first gesture as we watch her add many similar ones to it, confirming this as her style, but we are puzzled by the immediate appearance of the face. Natasha explains that whenever she tries to figure out what she is drawing she starts with human faces; it is her habitual way of getting under way. Then, as she elaborates the face with some of her prepared colors and similarly elaborates the surfaces of the leaves, she reveals that there is a deeper concern at work: to make a connection between nature and humans by adding heads, which "define the image through a human lens".

To this concern we may add two purely formal ones: some of the existing colors need to be made consistent with the palette (the white reflections on the leaves need to be removed, for example), and some empty spaces need to be filled. With this three-fold program—the word "program" is ours and is applied only in retrospect—she can proceed rapidly and consistently for the one and a half hours it takes her to finish the image. She sets down some of her touches with only partial opacity, revealing in this way both the shape underneath and some of the color. With the same sensitivity, she will later superimpose persimmons on faces, thus uniting fruits and humans.

Ultimately she will have added several faces to the composition and duplicated the persimmon four times, treating them all with the same colors and brush strokes; the brush strokes themselves will be of similar length and breadth. She will be conscious of pattern and abstraction, layering her various colors repetitively. (She will remark, however, that she preferred to stay halfway between the image and her transformations, adding that it would have been easy to erase every-thing and make something up—but that this way the image had some influence on her work. She had made an existing image "more organic by making it more spiritual—a kind of hallucination.") The accumu-lated brush strokes, the repeated shapes and colors, the loose manner of working, all lend her finished image an exceptional unity.

Discussing the painting with her immediately afterwards, we dis-cover that Natasha is concerned with the distance between computers and creativity—between the left brain and the right brain, in her words—and that the issue for her in making the image was reaching a balance between the computerized photo and an abstract, expression-istic, personal view of it. On that score she feels satisfied. But she soon shifts to another issue, that of unity of being; she remarks that as far as trees and humans go, "there is no difference between us as human beings and other life forms we consider less intelligent. I guess we're all pieces of fruit." Now a surprisingly broad unity is on the table, global and perhaps immanent, and our subject is as surprised as we. We ask her whether the image is related to her life in any way, and she says, laughing, " … I don't know how relevant this is, but my parents grow fruit, so I've grown up surrounded by fruit trees. Maybe that's why I chose the image in the first place … ." She adds that they have a lemon and avocado farm, and recalls, "it always amazed me in so much of my work that a lot of what I try to get across has to do with how I've been raised. A lot of my writing and my art work is connected in a deeply ingrained respect for cultivating life."

Her discovery seems akin to a breakthrough in psychotherapy. It is now clear that the connection between persimmons and heads, and between all creation animate and inanimate, is a deeply personal one. She is well aware of the desire for unity as impelling her work. But what gives it its relentless and repetitive character, and what is its connection to the fruit farm?

Natasha is the first of three surviving children, and except for moving away to college, has lived on the farm all her life, as have her two brothers. Her parents are still married, "pretty happily," she thinks, and her father tends to the farm while her mother combines the roles of mother, housewife, caretaker of the farm animals—and painter. I shall return to that in a moment.

She describes her father as nice, and also very introverted and shy; he is so protective of the farm that he can be rude, without realizing it, to people who happen by or come to solicit. His life is circumscribed by his farm and focused on his family, "especially my two brothers, because I think he feels like I have gotten so much from my mother from pursuing art, that I think he has trouble relating to me." She adds, "I wish I were closer to my dad, but he's a very hard person to be close to; my friends describe him as really uptight." Her father is in fact a pack rat who has lived in the house all *his* life and never let anything go; his office is so packed with things that one cannot even see the window, and he has the whole ranch programmed on a computer system. He is so secluded in his own world that he never even leaves the ranch; and his idea of meditation is to get out and work on his tractor and spray weeds. Although she resembles him in being introverted, the resemblance seems to end there.

Where her father is distant in general, and distant particularly from his artistic daughter, her mother is gregarious and open to all sorts of intimate communication. Her daughter admires her highly: she is very funny, does not always care what comes out of her mouth, and yet is amazingly competent in all that she undertakes and cares for. It is almost as if Natasha were puzzled by how a person so open and loose can be so effective. "She has a lot of friends and people who really love her, because she is so outgoing and so funny and really, really naive in many ways." Natasha explains that her mother is uninterested in such abstract matters as politics; she is down-to-earth instead, both in the literal sense of enjoying getting dirt between her fingers and the metaphorical one of being closely focused on her painting. In fact, her landscape painting has been a success, with her canvases being sold through a gallery, as well as an unexpected source of freedom. Now that the children are all in school she can leave the family periodically, for weeks at a time, to go painting elsewhere in California or in Europe. (The father feels cheated by this, but he is not strong enough to object.)

We can now return to Natasha's description of her purpose in creating her image of the fruit tree. She had explained that she wanted to create a balance between the computerized and the creative, and her description of her diametrically opposed parents tells us that the explanation was quite deeply personal. It is no mere balance; it is a balance between the distant, computer-organized father and the earthy, expressive, and artistic mother that she seems to seek. We think we can go further: more than finding the balance, she seeks to produce it. After saying that she did not understand how they got together as a couple, she adds, "they have always used me as a middle person. My dad would come to me and say, 'your mother is driving me crazy and she's pissed off at me,' and I would usually say, 'I think she's mad because she doesn't understand this aspect of you, and I can understand.' " The achievement of balance was a responsibility placed squarely on her shoulders early on.

But her purpose seemed to go deeper still—to portray the unity of the animate and inanimate, to show how we are all pieces of fruit. This is a deeper and less accessible level, and to describe it we may have to be content with a plausible guess; and as with the other subjects, a hint may be found in the state of her intimate relationships. Natasha tells us that she had isolated herself from others in junior high school and high school by her work, and had had no romantic or sexual relationships; even now she is only at the first stage of interest in a particular man. Her longest relation in high school was with a boy with whom she had wonderful intellectual conversations and a very intense spiritual connection. But reflecting on it she asks, "I wonder if we were trying to create something that was lacking between us using things like meditation," and so suggests at least a lack of emotional investment and perhaps

Figure 65. Temple Cluster

a missed physical contact as well. Even now she could not commit herself to a close relationship: "I am not at that point in my life right now".

Natasha puts everything into art. She makes clear that her artistic purpose is connected with integrating that which was too disparate, and illustrates better than any theoretical discussion could what is meant by the psychoanalytic notion of sublimation. And yes, the parents' fruit farm is the sublimation's site and metaphor.

TEMPLE CLUSTER

The image made by the man I call Evan is also unusually harmonious and unified, and it is filled with interesting tensions and carefully woven continuities; abstract yet suggesting the underlying landscape, it challenges the viewer to look hard. It was conceived in a manner suggesting the absolute primacy of style—a style chosen as a challenge to Evan's already considerable competence—yet it revealed a preoccupation with the substance of his life. The preoccupation revealed itself to Evan as he worked, and, through his articulate and voluble comments, to us.

His very choice of original image was based in style. *Hillside*—the arid landscape without sky but with one intrusive, pink house—had no form of its own, and it was enclosed, but it had interesting flat textures and allowed ample room for opening it up.[3] He was aware from the start of a wish to limit the number of colors, just as he intended to do with a projected series of paintings in which a limited palette would challenge him to construct space purely through color. His model in this was Richard Diebenkorn, whose abstract Ocean Park series alternated small areas of intense density with big, nearly monochromatic open spaces. So he explored color choice first, settling on a subtle mustard yellow, and painted a large, scraggly shape with it in the upper right corner. Thereafter he chose his colors almost solely from the image itself—a procedure which eventually created the cool, restrained harmonies of the finished picture.

Attending to linear connections between parts of the picture, Evan highlighted some of the roads with red-brown; then, finding the mustard patch too dense, he erased part of it; and finding the lower right corner too dark and dense, he altered its color and texture with several

---

[3] Evan is the only subject who responded to the possibilities we had seen in the image when we chose to include it. The few others who chose to work with it generally used it as a mere background for material they drew or pasted on top.

filters. He commented that the picture as it exists wants to scatter, and that he will try to integrate it with itself. He explained that he is very aware of weight and balance, and that he welcomes the opportunity to transplant elements from one part of the picture to another.

Suiting deed to the word, he turned to the pink house and copied and transplanted it, first into the upper right corner, later into the lower right corner. He smudged the edges of the transplant "to get rid of the stubbornness of those lines; lines are great, but they think the whole world revolves around them ... . They're like people, let's say; [I want to] make them incorporate other things into themselves." Then picking a blue pigment from the picture, he drew the broad winding shape that eventually came to resemble a river, and said, "It's like breaking down the firmness of that whole space there, making it pliable". Later he explained that the blue was a risk; he had been avoiding blue recently because it evoked water, sky, and the unconscious, and made him feel too calm.

Now Evan finally felt deeply engaged with the process and was ready to let go of what he called his conservatism; picking a neon green, he drew a broad, sloppy line with it (which he later erased), commenting that he was now at the point where he likes to be in a painting—fully engaged in the landscape, really feeling it, letting it have an effect on him. From this point on his descriptions were more vivid, more haptic—and more like comments on human relationships. In his words, the full response to landscape becomes like the trust one forms in a person as he becomes absorbed in him; the response to both is like a "full [kinesthetic] feel for the wholeness of the person". The response to a particular shape might reveal the painter's body, as his own liking for oak trees revealed his sense of himself as "tall and thin and lithe and slow". The response to converging lines might be a feeling of pressure at the point of intersection; and the sense of translucent surfaces, so much like Diebenkorn's "subverted" layers of color, was almost like not repressing a memory, letting what is underneath breathe through.

He finished the painting—the word is appropriate, because that is how he conceived it—by duplicating some of the mustard yellow from the upper right into two places on the left, fuzzing them up by hand, and unifying the texture of the image with a successive application of several filters. He did leave the pink house untouched, however. Asked if he wanted to name the picture, he was reluctant at first, but then said, Temple Cluster.

Commenting on the session right afterward, he made clear that his entire intention had been, as it is with his other work, to integrate the fluid, organic shapes with the more rigid, angular lines. Here, he wove "a web structure around the original pink temple, which for me was a real structural starting point ... . My initial gestures were going out from the temple, then it gradually became a working back inward ... . So I feel like it has certain elements of a balance that I look for."

But more than balance was at stake; that much became clear as Evan warmed up to the task of talking about the meaning of the painting for him. Painting for him is an accumulation of intimate influences: "the physical building of the colors and the transparency really hits me, because as we grow, we don't forget what happened to us. And just these subverted layers are somehow physical actualizations of those fundamental experiences of our lives ... . That light [on the original pink house] could be something more Freudian, like the relationships to my parents; it could be more spiritual—a relationship to the energy of life as I feel it; or maybe a relationship that I had, somebody I liked ... . Why was I interested in putting the temple in three different places?" Evan asked the question perhaps rhetorically, but was serious about suggesting the depth of meaning here: what is at stake in his manner of painting is a portrayal of his relationships. It is a portrayal whose details remained obscure until his final interview.

There was one other level of meaning of which Evan was aware now. Since he had been of two minds about using the calming color blue, we asked him if he ever used his work to create a calm space. He said he did. "What I realized with my work is that it's like creating an environment. I was thinking at one point in my life of making a chamber that's kind of misty and filled with purple light—maybe that's some kind of womb image, some kind of safe place ... . A painting can make an environment, not just a landscape kind of visual environment, but a very kinesthetic kind of environment." His painting, then, creates a safe space at the same time as it explores relationships.

The final interview, conducted by a different member of the research team, clarified the origins of both these concerns. Early on, Evan brought up his memory of his parents' divorce. When he was seven, his father returned from two long trips abroad and then moved away again for a year to write a book. His mother tried to get him to come back, especially for the sake of Evan and his sister, and then announced that she wanted a divorce. The father did come back in response to this and Evan's next vivid memory is of his father saying, "your mom and I have something to tell you," and being sat down to hear what that was. He started crying, but soon enough his mother told him that he would get used to it—and his defenses started kicking in. He refused to trust people or become close to them, and withdrew into himself until his junior year in high school, when he first threw himself into art.

He and his sister lived mostly with their mother after that, but they did visit their father for parts of the summer, and even spent one year with him. His sister developed an eating disorder and hypochondriasis; he took the divorce somewhat better, but only by convincing himself that it was the proper thing to do, not complaining even to himself, and becoming stoic "so that it wouldn't hurt so bad". The worst part of the whole period of traveling back and forth was all the time spent in airports: "we would say good-bye to our mom for the summer, and then we would be saying good-bye to our dad from the other end, ... and I remember that when I would go to the airport it was always pretty traumatizing."

His father was always a distant, emotionally inaccessible man whose involvement was elsewhere than with his children, and after the divorce, when he traveled back and forth on various assignments, he became even more emotionally closed; but Evan's need to make some connection with him did not lessen, and he makes the effort to do so even now, when they have little left in common.

He is, however, close to his mother and always has been. She went through a very emotional period during the divorce, providing for Evan's physical needs but not his emotional ones; yet he assumed something like a protective role toward her then and has retained it to this day. Her very traditional upbringing having failed her, she had to go through a period of growth, remake her life, make a new set of friends—and Evan talks of all this with a matter-of-fact acceptance. She has found a woman partner—a relationship that is good for both of them, much to his satisfaction—and Evan lived for several years surrounded by women. He sees himself as deeply pro-feminist and anti-sexist, and specifically identifies with his mother's patience, self-denial, even altruism; but this seems to him a mixed blessing, because he is also neither assertive nor commanding.

Nevertheless, his mother, now his confidante, was the first person to hear him talk about his problems when he first started thawing out in high school. It was a turning point: he took an art class, one in which he could do anything he wanted, and the freedom of movement and expression gave him precisely the sanctuary he needed. He dropped physics so he could take a triple art class and really work and concentrate, and then dropped mathematics so he could be in that art class almost every day. He says that he started talking more and opening up, and became ready to experience and feel things.

But high school was not a time of romantic or sexual exploration; he was too mistrustful of relationships for that. He did fall in love with a girl quite a bit younger than himself, but confined the relation to writing deep letters—which he now thinks must have scared her. In fact, he knows he was in his own little world. It was only after high school that he ventured out of it, became more deeply involved, and remained involved. But as much as he appreciates the growth that the young woman has made possible, he feels he is too close now and is trying to attenuate the romance and become mere friends. He had started out as a caretaker and neglected himself, and has come to realize that this has been the story of his life. At his request they see each other much less and are in his words "becoming very chaste together". This gives him the space he needs. He wishes to see other people and continues to dream of the right life partner; she would be—he laughs as he says this—"exactly like me except a woman, I guess"—and he means by this that she would be like him in compassion and acceptance. His favorite films are *Beauty and the Beast* (the Cocteau version) and *Wings of Desire*, which have in common so deep a love for a woman that the male figure, beast or angel, would die for her.

Perhaps it is understandable that he does not value sex highly. "Sex for me doesn't mean intercourse ... sexuality is a lot more than just body to body—things like cooking, like food, are very related to sexuality." While sexual contact is important in an intimate relationship, it is not central; it is sexual energy as a whole that he embraces.

Evan spoke so freely about all these matters that we feel we know him and can understand the wellsprings of his painting. The need to interconnect and balance everything on the canvas is in part aesthetic, but it is also a reflection of the painful dissolution of his family life; trying to bridge between distant poles is somewhat like attempting to establish a connection with his distant father, and more generally like the wish to reestablish the family's former togetherness. At the same time it cannot help but be a recognition of the actual separateness and the clearly remembered pain of separating. His wish for a close union remains as strong as are the defenses against it, and this is perhaps what gives his close-knit composition a particular poignancy. And yes, he, too sublimates in a classical sense: he deflects the energy held back from others into his work.

This cluster has given us a very clear sense of the psychological need to integrate the disparate parts of one's world and the pictorial means by which that may be attempted. *All four artists make clear their wish to tie together all aspects of their image, as they reveal the personal world that needs integrating.* One artist already feels genuinely connected with nature, parents, and brothers, but needs to experience and reproduce the connection as he works; another connects her feminine expressiveness with her masculine control; still another tries to unite the parts of her past that are too antithetical and chooses fruit as the universal symbol of that union; yet another tries to master the painful dissolution of his family. *All build on a firm basis of close ties once experienced*, and three—the exception being *Enchanted Sicily*—feel their attenuation. They do not have a romantic or erotic relationship—or have recently tried to change an erotic one into a chaste one—but they hold out the hope for one; creative work seems to fill the void at the moment. With their needs embodied so well in their art, perhaps we can understand why they seem content with their sublimations.

CHAPTER 9

Seventh Cluster

Abstraction, Avoidance, and the Search for Firm Boundaries

We turn finally to a cluster that is defined by one dimension only: abstraction. The pictures here avoid both representation and narration, they were constructed by mechanical rather than hands-on methods, and their space is flat; all in all they seem more detached than anything else. In this they are unlike the pictures in any of the other clusters.

Fuzzy, for example (see Figs 66–72), abstracts the star gazer lily from the still life, alters its texture and color altogether, and blends its boundaries with the flat, yellow background. *No* even wears the detachment on its sleeve, as it were: by its title it seems to negate all meaning and by its appearance to refuse all suggestion of material reality. Both *Choices* and *City of Dreams* (Fig. 73) are composed of flat patterns only; *Vein* makes patterns of the leaves that it had started with and flattens its formerly deep space by dividing it into distinct layers. *Highpass, Axon*, and *Frustrated* are all flatter than the original images and the latter (aptly titled) is constricted in its space and mechanically repetitive. Even the stylish and complex *Type on Flowers* (Fig. 74) divides its space into clearly defined layers.

Unlike the images in cluster 4, which share a hint of abstraction, these do not strike one by their purposeful denseness, and unlike the formal ones of the preceding chapter they do not seem concerned with composition. My primary task is then to explain the need to abstract, and, as I present the individual painters, to understand the particular ways of abstracting which are as important to each person as the general need to abstract is to the group: the blurriness of *Vein*, the constriction of *Frustrated*, the merging of boundaries in *Type on*

Flowers or the appearance of a realistic flower in *City of Dreams*, for example.

One is inevitably reminded, as I said in Chapter 1, of one of the pioneers of pure abstraction in painting—of abstraction that got as far away as it was possible to go from the suggestion of human substance— Piet Mondrian. Peter Gay (1976) has given us a picture of him as avoiding human contact in his life and, in his art, the slightest suggestion of contact through curvilinear form. Can the predominance of abstraction here reflect the same dynamics? We shall see that it does; among their other characteristics, our painters avoid the emotional and fleshy stuff of life. We shall find, however, that their very style—which is aware of the expressive meaning of boundaries—also reflects the importance of boundaries in their life.

THE PSYCHOLOGICAL PROCESS SEEN INDIVIDUALLY

Let us begin with the unusual **Fuzzy**. Because the painter preferred not to give her image a name, the title is ours, but it is one she did not find unacceptable. We were impressed by the last-minute blurring of the boundaries of the lily, the last act in a series of operations by which the still life was abstracted, transformed, and eventually simplified. A dancer rather than an art student, she had no clear intention at first but experimented instead; she tried some of the most radical filters, put dots of various bright colors on top of the flowers, and drew smiling

Figure 66. Fuzzy

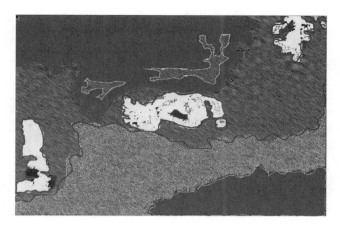

Figure 67. No

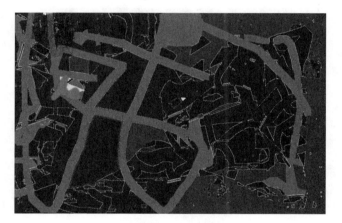

Figure 68. Choices

Figure 69. Vein

Figure 70. Highpass

Figure 71. Axon

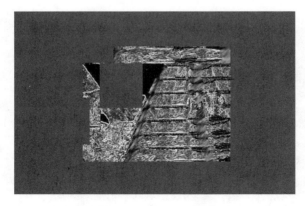

Figure 72. Frustrated

faces. She generally attended to one part at a time—the flowers in particular—and then, dissatisfied with the picture as a whole, changed her mind and turned toward the lily. She painted a mustard-yellow outline around it, adding her initials which she then removed, then wrenched it from the rest of the composition, enlarged it, replaced the background with an expanse of the same sharp yellow, and textured the body of the flower. As a final gesture, she blurred its outlines by hand.

In her life, what leaps to the eyes is the question of boundaries: her mother was at once intrusive and neglectful, her father emotionally distant, and there was no guidance or discipline; the parents smoked pot to hide the problems between them. She is enmeshed with her mother even now, and the parents are in turn enmeshed with her boyfriend. Because he had been kicked out by another woman, they have let him move in with them, and she sees this as inappropriate in part because he has taken her place, in part because she and he are neither emotionally nor physically close. She, too, likes to erase boundaries between herself and others quickly, however, but invariably comes to fear losing herself ("I get really close, and then I start to feel that I don't know who I am"); the result is that she is wary of closeness. The flower in her picture is her: "yes, extending out, penetrating, with energy coming out, like the beginning of a relationship."

If boundaries are *Fuzzy's* overriding issue, and blurring them both the temptation and the fear, they are also the issues of the woman who created **Type on Flowers** (Fig. 74). Her multiple layering of the image, her blurring of the flowers' boundaries, her superimposition of names on each other, all serve the same purpose aesthetically and psychologically. The daughter of parents who never touched each other, she is working on separating herself from her dependent father and managing the question of merging and separation from her boyfriends; indeed, one of them had wounded himself with a gunshot when she separated from him years before, and now wants to return. Her image is elegant, however, her life complex, her insights deep, and we shall reserve a fuller discussion of her for a later part of the chapter.

The young man who created **No** is not an art student, but he does take a careful three hours to create his picture, both uncertain of what he wants to do and unable to let it go. Without a plan, he nevertheless starts right in, tracing the outlines of the mountains in the *Hillside* landscape, drawing a number of small lines under magnification, and smudging a little here and there. He comments, "that's kind of cool; how long do I get to do this?" We sense that he is emotionally detached, even though he traces minutely around the outlines of the original shapes and erases all careless gestures, no matter how small.

He seems contradictory in his attitude—complaining at one moment
that the computer doesn't work for him but claiming at another that
the process is really easy—and in a way self-defeating: some of his
interventions are tiny and have little effect.

The son of a "marshmallow, wishy-washy" father with a mushy
sense of humor and an embarrassingly loud mother, he is now equally
distant from both. His own diction is voluble and complex, but often
without direction, just as his picture of his parents' expectations of him
is vague and his idea of his own goals inchoate ("I am headed for happiness"). In his relation to his woman friend he is distant physically
("we always talk about the fact that we feel we don't even have bod-
ies"), and in his tastes in film he is abstemious ("if there was a kissing
scene in a movie, I would have to get it over with"). He says that in
his life he plans too much and fails to enjoy the moment, although in
making his picture (perhaps liberated by the free and merely symbolic
task) he does not plan at all. His abstractness is an avoidance of contact,
of romance, of dependence.

The picture **Choices** is deceptively incisive and purposeful. It
evolved in fact without a plan, from the complex and disorderly
Garden photograph, and reveals a very similar psychology behind its
abstractness. Starting out by selecting areas of the picture with the
Magic Wand (which will mark out an area by color and value, not
always in predictable ways), the young man poured various opaque
colors into them, making them flat and hard-edged. He would change
the colors, define more areas and pour colors into those, move areas
around, rotate them and duplicate them, and eventually find a way to
draw broad lines that look like roads on a map. Finally, trying and then
rejecting a number of the filters, he wound up with a patterned picture
that, to our eyes, had much to recommend it aesthetically. It had been
done mostly by hands-off operations, and was so far from its starting
point that one could wonder what role the starting point had played at
all. In his subsequent interview he was reserved and warned us that he
might have trouble answering some of our questions, but he did in fact
talk about himself clearly.

He described his father as rational, intelligent, and as the structure
on which the family rested (or the family that would have been had the
parents not divorced); curiously, the description itself is vague, in that
the father presumably does "a lot of stuff", and right now is building
an airplane. He began to speak of his mother by saying "I don't know
how to describe my mom either", but added soon enough that she was
impulsive, intuitive, and crazy, and was capable on short notice of
taking herself and the children to France for a trip. She had been a kind

of hippie, had dropped out of society, and still moves around a lot. His account of his childhood is in fact unbelievably confusing, at least as much to him as to us; he has lived in many places and with various assortments of adults, suffered the occasional intrusion of his father into their living arrangements, again with little structure or discipline or clear parental expectations, and has comparably unclear goals for himself now. He describes his intimate relationships as "crazy, confused—I've never [really] had a relationship". He adds that he cannot understand women; they seem totally crazy to him, and too needy; and as to sex, he didn't think it was important and had in fact hoped we would not bring it up. As much as he talks of structure in this picture and in his other art works, he has difficulty formulating goals and even in his speech wanders and contradicts himself. Clearly, he, too, abstracts in order to avoid contact. And by assembling clearly bounded areas of color in an unplanned manner, he can construct a clear product.

The woman who drew **Vein**, an art student, layered her picture somewhat as *Type on Flowers* had, and she, too, likes to add words to her pictures to make them more interesting. But the only word she added here is "Blur", and its fuzzy outline is made consistent with its meaning. *Blur* was in fact her title, but we needed to distinguish her picture from another one by the same name, and chose a name that reflects the dark blue veins which trace the ribs and outlines of the leaves; ours does not evoke her meaning, however. Choosing the Leaves photograph "because it was the most abstract" to begin with, she abstracts the left half of the image with a filter that selects out edges and transforms colors, and begins to work by hand on individual leaves in the right half, outlining them in different colors, "just picking leaves randomly—I don't have a system". She subdivides the picture into rectangles, whose surface she transforms with other filters, and draws a circle into which she inserts the word "blur", all of which she blurs in turn.

She grew up in a commune—her parents still live in it—with little discipline, direction, and minimal expectations. She describes her father in vague terms (tall, blond, spiritual, into being busy, and with an unclear occupation), and sees her mother as overly protective of her, even obsessed. At the same time the mother is wishy-washy (as *No's* father had been), passive and limp ("if I told her to jump off a cliff, she would"). This mutual intrusiveness results in a physical distance from people. She has not had any longterm intimate relationships, keeps those that she has fairly distant, finds sex not crucial, and would consider it ideal for her man to be her best friend like some of her best girl friends are; appropriately enough, a recent comedy she had enjoyed is "Boys on the Side". Like the painter of *Fuzzy*, she makes boundaries her main issue, and, even more than she, reflects her directionless childhood in the diffusion of her thinking, unable to decide between alternatives: is Boys on the Side a romantic comedy, she asks? "I guess it is, well, no, it's not, well, it kind of is". For her, abstraction is a kind of avoidance, too, and blurring a way of managing unclear boundaries.

The picture **Highpass** is abstract in a different way: while retaining the leafy character of the original, the image maker emphasizes the leaves' outlines (by using the Find Edges filter, like so many of the painters in this cluster; its very title presumably connects with the question of boundaries that is so prevalent here). He simplifies the background and adds elements from the still life photo. The result is fairly flat as well, and distinctly patterned, perhaps a shade sad and listless with its grey-violet tone. The young man who drew it is somewhat taciturn, more intellectual than artistic. Like all the participants so far, he is the son of an uncommunicative, unemotional father, but unlike them, he has an unemotional mother, too; he sees himself as unemotional in turn. With each parent remarried after their early divorce, he has lived with his mother most of his life; even so, he is more distant from her than from him. When growing up he preferred the company of his friends and later of his little brother, or he stayed in his room a lot, and now he gets together with his family only about once a year, and at that only for a few days. His present relationships are comparably sparse; he has had only one romantic involvement— a very brief one—and seems to find all romantic possibilities turning into mere friendships. His speech is, however, precise, although succinct and labored, as if it cost him some effort to answer questions about emotional matters. So his manner of abstracting is different: it is directed at avoiding contact, not at confusing reality. He blurs nothing in his speech or in his picture.

Nor does the young woman who created **Axon** (our title, reflecting the transformation of the star gazer lily). With a passion for flowers and a preference for working on the separate parts of the still life rather than on more connected pictures, she proceeded—also without a plan—to transform them one at a time, each differently and at first with filters (the Find Edges filter appeared here, too). Whenever she chose a filter, she would reset its parameters for the strongest effects simply by choosing the highest numbers available, without knowing ahead of time what it would look like. When she was done with the flowers, she filled in the background with well rehearsed squiggles, leaving no voids or areas of respite.

The daughter of divorced parents—an uninvolved, passive and shy father, who complicated the family's life by having children by

other women, and an overprotective, achieving and intrusive mother—
she is not close to either parent; if anything, she is closer to her father
by virtue of avoiding her mother. She is somewhat strained when talking
of her relationships with men; there have been few and none of them
have been close. Unlike our other image makers in this cluster she
felt that her parents did have expectations for her future, but she
nevertheless has few goals for herself and avoids thinking about topics
that are complex or emotional. Once again, the style is avoidant.

The picture **Frustrated** suggests constriction at least a much as
abstraction: the whole is squeezed into a small, irregular space, with
the architectural elements of the original image—Temple—stretched
and filtered and piled up in a pyramidal shape. Its maker, a young man,
worked repetitively by outlining details, altering their shape, replicat-
ing and multiplying them, and essentially making a kind of collage; he
was both systematic and precise. Unlike the other participants, he had
a plan from the start: "I was going to make a weird, repetitive, temple
façade thing", an image related in spirit to his other art work, which is
"about memory and obsessive engagement in something". As an example, he describes a box he was making "that is completely covered in
nails, with points sticking up ... where it is rows and rows of nails over
the whole thing, and then I am going to wrap it in string, so that you
can look at it and say, 'that is really somebody obsessed'; ... it relates
to the way religion functions in society."

He shares with the other members of this group a distant father—in
this case a formal, intellectual and intimidating one—and has always
felt inhibited in all his actions: "I always hung back and checked everything out before deciding." His mother is, however, a woman whose
efforts to become herself after the parents' divorce he appreciates: he
admires her liking to do weird things, have fun, and above all be emotionally honest. Nevertheless, apart from that similarity, he is the kind
of person who needs order and ritual to keep him organized, whether in
repairing objects over and over again until he gets it right, in seeing religious rituals as psychologically nourishing, in having as his goal an
improvement in his concentration and discipline, or in understanding
sex as a "consummation ritual". He suggests a strong capacity to identify with his parents' prohibitions when he describes his reaction to
their disappointment at his having had friends over to the house when
they were away: he decided never to have people over again. He had
never thought of his parents as a unit—they met very young and
behaved more as friends than as lovers—and he, too, is distant in his
relationships. Although there is some avoidance in his style, too, we
would emphasize his control through ritual and obsessiveness.

The picture called ***City of Dreams*** (Fig. 73) was produced by an artist who, like most of the other painters in this cluster, worked without a plan but with a repetitive process he hoped would arrive at something satisfactory. Somewhat like *Type on Flowers*, he has difficulty in separating himself from his parents, particularly from his father, himself an artist. Boundaries therefore come up in his picture as they do in his life, and because they are a complex matter, and because as in the painter of *Type* a well practiced style connects with deeper, personal needs, we shall reserve him, like her, for a more detailed discussion.

THE PSYCHOLOGICAL DYNAMICS OF
THIS CLUSTER

What leaps to the eye is the distance that all these individuals maintained from others, and *the embodiment of that distance in the final appearance of the images and in the process by which they were made—the one being abstract, the other being hands-off, relying predominantly on the mechanical filters*. I can now add that even those who contemplated a career as artists, or had one already (with the exception of the maker of *City of Dreams*), were interested in design or commercial art—careers which emphasize control and usefulness over emotional expression. I concluded that their pictorial abstraction was an avoidance of the emotional stuff of life. One might say that, like Mondrian, they avoided the fleshy side of life as well. In response to our question about the importance of sex in their lives they presented a dramatic contrast to the other highly controlled cluster, the one that had produced dense images (Chapter 6): all but one here said that sex was unimportant, or qualified their answer in a way that distanced them from it (it's an "urge" or a "consummation ritual"). The one exception (*City of Dreams*), who values both sex and love, nevertheless has a long history of merely brief relationships.

If all the painters abstract in order to maintain an emotional distance, *they also seem engaged in maintaining or defining their boundaries*. Some painters came from families that were mixed up in their membership while others lived with parents who were inconsistent in their own thinking, unconcerned about discipline, or intrusive into their child's space and thinking. Perhaps as a consequence, we also found that their life goals were inchoate. The effect of this on their style was to emphasize boundaries. The painters of *Fuzzy* and *Vein* revealed the vague boundaries between themselves and their parents in their own wooly images, while six of the seven others on the contrary emphasized the edges of their objects by giving them sharp outlines; they did this by cutting and reassembling, or using the "Find Edges" filter. Because the clarity they achieved was in some ways without pictorial purpose—their images were assembled or transformed piecemeal—the hardness of the edges seems merely the obverse of the same dynamics. The last painter, *Type on Flowers*, actively tackled the issue of boundaries in a manner more commensurate with its insistent role in her life: she layered and merged, as well as blurring.

If this is what our painters have in common, they are also individuals with unique histories and varying talents and particular solutions to the matter of closeness and boundaries. It is to two such people, both older and both artists, that we turn.

CITY OF DREAMS

The painting's title is no accident: it indicates Ron's desire to actualize his dreams as an artist. Ron, of course, is a pseudonym, and he is in his mid-forties, earning his living in a skilled manual occupation and working as an artist as much as he can. As constant as these activities are, he does feel that he still has a "pilot light on in his life and that the jets have not kicked in"—that he has never known his purpose and his direction. There is a woman in his life right now, as there have been before, but he spends much of his time by himself and lives alone with his cat. He knew one of the experimenters and volunteered to participate out of curiosity.

Starting with the still life, he quickly disposed of most of the flowers, selected some remaining fragments of shapes and began to duplicate them over the surface of the picture. By cutting and repetitive assembling, in other words, he started not so much painting as composing: his surface was balanced at all times but without an idea of what he wanted, and indeed he wished to delay finding out as long as he could. The abstract shapes with small, rectangular dots did, however, begin to look like a cityscape once they had been set down enough times, and he then drew straight lines around some of them to make sure they resembled buildings. With this setting established, he believed he saw the shape of a woman in one of the faint circles, and, happy to add a human element to the picture, he duplicated it several times. As a last flourish, he went into the upper left corner and used the erasing tool to uncover the flower that had been there all the time.

He worked quickly but took over two hours, and the process seemed somewhat aggressive to us in its rapid obliterations. We were

Figure 73. City of Dreams

not convinced he had no idea where he was going: saying in the middle of the work, as he did, "I am working with the idea of a cityscape" seemed to be revealing a clear and perhaps well established intention, one which he may not have been aware of at first. Be that as it may, he did balance aggression with reparation, in reintroducing a human "element" and a full-blown, realistic flower. We shall soon see its meaning.

In the subsequent interview he talked freely and, if anything, at considerable length. His father is a retired commercial artist and cartoonist, a quiet man in good spirits most of the time—different from Ron in his temperament, since Ron has always been rebellious—but like Ron, of course, he has his artistic desires and pursuits. Asked about his present relation to him, Ron said that it was very good, and imperceptibly veered in an unusual direction indicating a certain enmeshment or at least need for reparation: as a vegetarian, Ron thought he ought to help his asthmatic father by changing his diet, and he succeeded fully. Both parents are now vegetarians, both meditate, and the asthma has disappeared. I do think he was still answering the question, but he was also showing a controlling concern for his parents and a propensity to meander.

His mother had been the authority in the house, or at least the person charged with discipline, and Ron did his best to make her life difficult: he preferred to run out and play, always pushed the limits, in short "bucked the system", while his mother attempted to reign him in. She was also a good mom in that she handled the household well, prepared good meals, and made sure everyone had clean clothes, clean bedding, and a roof over their heads. Now they get along best at a distance (although he leaves room for hope because they have been meditating), and much of his criticism is muted; he realizes that he resembles her physically and that he is somewhat like her in being critical and emotional. He is in fact more closely connected with her than with his father, because his father is closed in on himself. Ron's attempts to break through—indirect though they may be, as by bringing him a Robert Bly tape on father/son relationships—have met with only the most limited success.

One may presume that his relation to his mother has influenced his relations with his lovers, but it is his father who has been crucial in determining his sense of himself as an artist. At peace now, the father was disappointed in his main wish, which was to become a cartoonist; he had too few cartoons published to be able to quit the job he didn't like very much. When he was young there had been no doubt in his mind that he was going to be a successful cartoonist—he was a wonderful artist and had full confidence in his art—but it didn't work out.

That Ron feels his father's failure acutely is clear from the way this comment had bubbled up: he had in fact been asked about the parents' relationship when they were younger. Reminded of that question, he returns to it, but is again diverted by his concern over his own role in that relationship: unlike other children, he says, he has worked out his relation to them, which makes their relationship good: "I really do feel very complete with them and they seem happy with each other."

Rebellious, then, he had to strike out on his own and in spite of his father's wishes he quit college after a mere semester; thereafter he felt a challenge to prove his father wrong and earn adequate money without the education. He also rebelled against his father's wanting him to paint representational art; he recalls his father saying to him, "When are you going to paint something I can recognize?" *Doing abstract work became a way of rebelling, of asserting himself.* Even when he saw a figure of a woman in the present picture, so resistant was he to revealing this side of his art that he did not want to admit it to the experimenter.

I had mentioned a need for reparation in connection with the restitution of the realistic rose and also with his concern for his parents' diet. Perhaps the two ways of expressing it can be linked now: if the reparative impulse concerns his father's career as well, then the realistic flower—almost an after-thought—might be a bow to the recognizable painting the father did and wanted his son to do. The idea is not far-fetched, if we are to judge by Ron's reaction to it when, at his request, we met with him to discuss our findings and interpretations. He accepted it as probable, and he then accepted another suggestion: that in the image he made for us he moved in and out of emotional closeness, with the abstract elements being distant and rebellious, and the realistic and human ones close and accepting.

In his present intimate relationships he vacillates similarly. Describing the role of love, he says that it is the difference between life and death; without love he would "leave this body pretty quick". Sex, too, is very important, although he now finds that being able to be close, to cuddle and massage, to combine intimacy with sexuality, is more important than when he was younger. I have no reason to doubt his word, but I must also note that his relationships have been many and quite short—that on the whole they would last about two years and soon be replaced, and that he seems to be more in love with love than in love with people. Only lately has he allowed more time to elapse between women. Sometimes reparative impulses get in his way: he finds it easier to care for his partners than to allow them to care for him. As I have said, he lives alone, and he certainly has no thought of marriage or children.

Some aspects of his present life, as with most people, and of his career as an artist, are a compromise. He says that unlike his father he has little self-confidence as an artist; he moves forward, he likes some of the things he does artistically, but feels that he needs to be pushed—perhaps by being recognized. "I have never really known my purpose and direction, ... I will try landscaping or electronics or inventing, ... but I would like to actualize my dreams of living as an artist." I may add that perhaps his understandable ambivalence about his father's success as a cartoonist, and his insistence on realistic representation, might be inhibiting as well.

TYPE ON FLOWERS

The young woman who produced *Type on Flowers* also faced the challenge of combining aesthetic concerns with psychological ones. In her mid-thirties and employed as a commercial artist, "Laura" was also an acquaintance of one of the experimenters and was as motivated by curiosity about herself as was Ron. Since art was her profession, the balance of the artistic and the psychological may have been different: if anything, while working with us she felt more freedom than in her work.

Whether she began with ideas carried over from her work or with a fresh response to the flower still life is unclear to us, but she did blur the rose in the upper right corner early on, and did say soon that it was "not getting weird enough"—a statement she promptly incorporated into the picture. Blurring the rose suggests a personal meaning, as with other women who found the rose a reminder of conflicted sexuality, but the motto is definitely a fusion of personal meaning with a mode of working useful in her present job. She proceeded to create transparent layers, cut out portions of them to tilt and repaste onto the surface, wrote more messages, and merged names at right angles to each other. She would also obliterate the merging as an afterthought. At all times, she seemed aware of the aesthetic consequence of each gesture, and indeed the final result is elegant and formal.

Immediately after finishing her picture she tells us that she is happy with it, particularly with the layering: "I like merging various images; I think that it helps create edges or shapes that are less defined ... . I am usually attracted to obliterating things, ... to the fact that this is partly real but I distorted it a lot." In effect she herself defines two psychological issues that matter to her: merging with others and obliterating. She explains both quite readily. Turning to the experimenter, she says, "I went through a period when I cared a lot

Figure 74. Type on Flowers

about what you were thinking as I was going along ... where is the boundary between Me and the Other? To what extent do I give my power away or my self-image away to somebody else?" As she says this, she is aware of having crossed her name with that of the experimenter in the picture, as a sign of the wish to merge. But she also aware that superimposing type over an image, which distorts and obliterates, has an aggressive function. "I am very attracted to type as pattern. I have this feeling that making images that are distorted or twisted or weird is kind of like saying, no, fuck you. Not to you, but I think to my mom ... . My parents thought about themselves and their needs and had very little time for me or mine. My mother always redefined my feelings for me."

In this excerpt from the brief interview which followed the completion of the picture, Laura has told us as much as we would normally glean from the full personality interview of other participants, and interpreted it convincingly as well. Her two issues may well have a common origin—her resistance to contact, and the wish to merge, may both be effects of her mother's intrusiveness—but their stylistic effect is to negate by obliterating, and merge by combining and layering.

But more was to be revealed by Laura's later interview. Her father is a very dependent person, one who hovers around Laura and her mother whenever they are around. When she was younger he was away at work a lot, so it did not matter that much, but now it has become annoying. A person who smiles chronically, even when angry, he became a model for Laura and she came to hide much of herself from herself; yet, through therapy, she has become more real, more expressive, more independent. There is some sort of bond between them, she says, and she feels that her father cares about her and is the only person in the world who ever did. But she adds, "I don't think I have separated from him very well and a lot of the feeling that I get from him is that if only I would come home and live there, he would be happy ... . I don't need that kind of stuff, but at the same time I am very hooked in." We could only admire the clarity with which she described the enmeshment, its effects on her, and by implication its effects on her artistic style.

Matters were hardly better with her mother. An angry workaholic, she was avoided by the rest of the family; they were careful not to criticize, question, be angry—or be honest in any way whatever—because she could not take it. Not having a sense of self, as the family put it, she could not encourage anyone's success or independence; Laura and her siblings felt that they were to remain dependent on her and never leave. Critical and perfectionistic, she encouraged criticism and perfectionism in Laura; and yet she also encouraged an interest in the arts and music, which Laura can now value. Apart from the mother yelling at the father, the parents are estranged; Laura thinks they dislike each other. She has very little contact with either of them.

Like the other image makers in this cluster Laura recollects very little discipline and only the vaguest expectations for her future, but, unlike them, she is aware of having formed a strong conscience. She recalls the parents going away once and Laura throwing a wild high school party, with someone calling the police and the police calling the parents in turn; the parents "knew that we knew it was bad and we felt bad, so they really didn't punish us but they never ever went away again." (The young man who painted *Frustrated* recounted the very same experience and the very same appeal to conscience—and he added, "so it worked pretty well.") If both have a strong conscience, his is shown in his many inhibitions, while hers is shown in an oscillation between acting out, in her picture as in her life, and attempting to create an elegant wholeness.

Not in a relationship with any man at the moment, Laura nevertheless does value relationships with men and is trying to make them more equal and less dependent. Ready ever since her teens to sleep with a man right away, and feeling as a result that people wanted her for sexual reasons only, she is trying to let the kind of richness develop that comes from taking time. (She does in fact say that she has felt desired sexually since her childhood, and gives us a sense of deep anger at some unstated transgression of boundaries, however that may have happened.) Like the other members of the group, she can now say that sex is less important. But her desire for a close connection is unremitting: "I can feel insane if I don't feel connected to somebody."

I can now clear up a detail in her picture which might have gone unnoticed. She had begun by blurring the outlines of the rose in the upper right corner. She told us later that she keeps a rose in her freezer that was given to her recently by a former high school lover; this is the man who is trying to come back to her after all these years. She has every reason to feel ambivalent about it: sad, yes, but also wary, because he is the one who shot himself—making an obviously non-fatal wound—when they separated. She must feel that maintaining boundaries is a formidable task and perhaps a dangerous one.

I would add that she is not only open and clear about the more problematic parts of her life but also precise in her speech. She is willing to work hard with the interviewer and knows that if the interview were to continue, there would be much more to add, although it might take a long time to get the information out. If on a couple of occasions in the interview she lost track of the question, she nevertheless asked to be reminded. Reflecting what we think is a deep wound, she does, as she puts it, dissociate. It seems all the more of a tribute to her capacity for wholeness that she knows it, brings herself quickly back into focus—and when making art can produce an image that feels complete while revealing her full complexity.

This group, like the others but perhaps more simply and directly, leads us to the central role of relationships—remembered and actual—in guiding the hand of our image makers. It is as if their physical and emotional experience of avoidance became a governing metaphor for avoiding contact with their images, and as if, too, the question of the self's boundaries translated into a process by which they had to be managed in the creative act. How this happens is not clear, but I shall next look at all seven ways of making art from that point of view.

CHAPTER 10

Art Making, Maps of Interpersonal Space, and the World of Art

History tells us that art is the product of many needs and constraints, of which the personal ones are only a part. It is difficult to say what the relative importance of social requirements and individual ones might be—such as the need for a particular style to suit a particular epoch, as against the need for individual expression. Surely their relative importance varies with time and place, and equally surely both sets of determinants need to be taken into account. But in any given study, and in any given discipline, one has to select out the part one can illuminate, and in the present one I have made all the room I could for the contributions of personality. What I hope to have demonstrated here is that that contribution is both significant and understandable, even in individuals for whom art has become a discipline—and perhaps to have shown that the better it is understood, the more seriously it needs to be taken.

Looked at from within, the virtue of these results is that the relation between visual style and personal needs has been so consistent. Now it is appropriate to look at the results from without, from a slight distance and as much perspective as one can manage. To do that, I would like to look at the material in three ways. One is to abstract the five individual dimensions from the clusters in which they had appeared—since they were orthogonal to begin with—and look at them as if they were independent of their setting; this is a way of asking what are the sources of stylistic qualities such as "boldness" and "informality". Then I would like to return to the interpersonal world with which we started—the world of contact, of boundaries, of interpersonal coherence, and of connections to the past—and look at the results in its terms. Finally,

I would like to make an attempt to relate the seven art making styles to the public world of art, to see to what extent well known painters, or less well known but recognized ones, can fit our dimensions.

DIMENSIONS OF ART MAKING

In order to see how the images would cluster, we had to isolate orthogonal dimensions that would describe them adequately; in our sample, there were five. To have studied them independently, we would have had to use a different method, such as correlating them with measurable dimensions of personal functioning, and while this method would have been defensible, it would have lost the sense of configuration that I prefer. Configuration is present in the clusters themselves, thanks to the way they were constructed, and it is of course the fundamental form of the whole individual. A correlational analysis would have also masked the possibility that a given style may be the product of two quite different psychological processes. Now three of the five dimensions were embodied in two clusters each, which is to say that they generally took two different forms; if we now abstract them from the clusters, we will see if they embody multiple meanings.

Thus **timidity** is illustrated by the first and the fifth clusters. It refers to a kind of failure to stimulate a response in the viewer, thanks either to an absence of originality or an inability to arouse emotion. We have found timidity in the cluster that creates images from a reparatory wish for a better reality, and then again in the cluster that is motivated by perfectionism and an adherence to parental standards. Both predispositions seem inhibiting, but each in a different way, and we can suggest that timidity can have two meanings: it can result from the lack of inventiveness, perhaps because the reparatory wish is sentimental in nature and crowds out the search for form, or it can result from a fear of making mistakes.

Its opposite, **boldness**, is defined by originality and the ability to evoke a viewer's response, and it was seen in the third and fourth clusters. In cluster 3, we have seen boldness connected to readily available emotions, in particular anger, while in cluster 5, we saw the boldness as driven, persistent, perhaps obsessive. Once again we see an expanse of motives, ranging from something like emotional expressiveness to something more determined and cognitive; the first kind of boldness seems free, the second willful, and in the first case the images are vigorous, while in the second they are densely compacted. The first kind of boldness is emotionally direct, while the second kind is relentless and compelling.

The dimension of **flow** indicates a process that was seen to proceed relatively smoothly and an image that shows diffuseness and movement; it characterizes two clusters that appear quite distinct at first. One is the third cluster, which showed the boldness we have just discussed, and the other is the integrative, artistic, sixth cluster. If the first of these is expressive and emotionally free, the second is deeply motivated to integrate each image—to connect the masculine and feminine, for example, to reconnect with nature, and to reestablish the broken tie between the parents. The artists in the latter cluster also have the well practiced skill to do the integrating, and while they might be well have been free to work this way even in the absence of artistic experience, we must presume that practice helps. Either the mastery of a range of graphic gestures (and perhaps the practice of connecting them with ideas and images), or sheer availability of emotion, may be expected to create a certain flow in image making.

The absence of flow, on the other hand—a **saccadic** process—also reintroduces two clusters we have looked at already, but in a different context. The fourth cluster—driven, persistent, and obsessive—here joins the fifth cluster, which was perfectionistic. The images the two groups produce are done haltingly, and appear static, sharp, and focused. The willful boldness of cluster 4 can now be seen for its willfulness rather than for its boldness: too great an exercise of a conscious purpose has taken away from spontaneous flow. In cluster 5, however, it is perfectionism that inhibits the flow, just as it had inhibited originality earlier.

But perfectionism also has the virtue of focusing the individual's attention on form, so the **formal** dimension becomes embodied in the otherwise inhibited fifth cluster as well. At the cost of some loss of spontaneity, the image makers who identify with their parents' perfectionism also strive for form—but unlike the form of the artists in the sixth cluster, theirs is repetitive or dainty, imposed on the subject matter from without rather than being an inherent part of it. The artists in cluster 6, on the other hand, seem to create a formal surface that conveys its subject convincingly and even elegantly; form expresses and conveys the content rather than competing with it.

Informality returns us to the first cluster, whose wish-fulfilling or reparative desires, I had said, seemed to overwhelm any wish for more formally conceived compositions; we presumed that preoccupation with subject matter left little room for formal considerations. The other informal cluster, the second one, had a similar background of early pain, loss, or deprivation, but responded by downcast, angry feelings, and reflected their lack of connection with others in their disconnected forms. These seem to be two different processes: in the first, we saw form displaced by content, while in the second, the absense of form actually conveyed a lack of interconnection; informality in the first case was a matter of neglect, and in the second a matter of symbolizing formlessness.

Both **expansiveness** and **constriction** are, however, illustrated by only one cluster each, so we cannot broaden our understanding of them beyond what we have said already. Expansiveness was a matter of working with larger forms and an upbeat mood, and reflected reparatory wishes; constriction meant smaller forms and a downbeat mood, and reflected the artists' downcast lives. Mood, in other words, and mood alone, determined the breadth and feeling tone of the forms. And **abstraction**, too, was embodied in one cluster only, the seventh cluster, and in fact fully defined it. In their final form the images were well removed from their photographic or representational starting point; what was striking was that the process by which they had been produced was a mechanical, hands-off process, one that was bodily separated from the image. The images also emphasized boundaries, either by excessive sharpness or uniform fuzziness. On the one hand we saw the artists avoiding the emotional and fleshy side of life, which seemed a sufficient explanation for their abstractness, and on the other we saw them defining their boundaries, either by a woolly approach reminiscent of their parents' vague relation to them, or by the imposition of excessively sharp edges, or in a few cases by both.

If it is a reasonable rule in the psychological world that a given effect may have more than one cause, or to put in into the more familiar "in the world of reality ... overdetermination is the rule" (Freud, 1959), then we have found these aspects of image-making to be overdetermined; nothing could surprise one less. Indeed, if the situation were to be simpler, and each aspect of image making were to reflect one clear psychological need or predisposition only, we would be faced with two consequences, both undesirable for art: we would have removed all sense of awe or mystery from art, and we could use art as a diagnostic device. The one would remove one of art's reasons for being, and the other would make anyone attempting to make images too careful and defensive an artist. Some degree of revelation feels acceptable, but too much would leave us utterly transparent. Nothing reported here need raise that fear.

Now I return to the people we have studied and to the generalization I proposed at the outset. There I said that one's *image of interpersonal relationships is a kind of map by which aesthetic reality can be ordered and understood, and indeed ... the relationships one seeks to create between the elements of a visual image ultimately stand for one's interpersonal world.* Looking over all that we have seen, can it still be said that that describes the findings best? And what would be the relation of this formulation to other psychodynamic views of artistic endeavors?

BRINGING IT TOGETHER: IMAGES OF THE INTERPERSONAL WORLD

Any psychodynamic account of image making must situate itself in relation to two better known alternatives: the wish for reparation and the mechanism of sublimation. Of these, reparation is the less well known but it is an integral part of the Kleinian view of personality dynamics and it is a cornerstone of the theory of artistic creation (Segal, 1952). It refers to the wish to atone for aggressive wishes felt early in infancy and to re-create the objects that one's aggressive impulses are believed to have destroyed; by extension, it can refer to overcoming losses once sustained. We have had clear illustrations of this dynamic in our first cluster, where losses were clearly evident and where satisfying images were created to make up for them. One must, indeed, take the concept seriously, but paradoxically by doing so and finding evidence of it in one group of creators, one implies that it is not present in the others; in Kleinian theory, however, it is universal. Perhaps a process one takes seriously cannot be both real and universal at the same time.

Sublimation is intended as an equally general description of artistic creation, and as a concept it is the better known; it refers to a displacement of motives from the private, unacceptable realm to the public, acceptable one, and, in art specifically, giving attractive and understandable form to what had been private and perhaps incomprehensible (Freud, 1908). One easily thinks of passionate love being sublimated into charitable work—or, in these findings, of the wish for making one's most intimate reality whole being sublimated into well integrated compositions. Such instances of sublimation are clear enough, but, as with reparation, the clearer they are the less universal they become.

This might displease the theorists who would prefer to protect the two concepts' universality, but it does not seem an unsatisfactory outcome to me: universal explanations run the risk of saying both too much and too little at the same time. And although I integrate the reparation and sublimation into my own thinking, I also realize that they only describe motives—the wishes and impulses to do something— rather than the form that the motives will take. Perhaps what is needed is something more descriptive.

This is why I think of the image making we have looked at here as a symbolic process—a process that orders or gives symbolic represen- tation to the individuals' interpersonal world, or reveals the represen- tations that are already there. A symbolic process has the advantage of representing motives as well as ways of dealing with them, and offers a more specific account of differences between individuals. To see the findings this way may require no more than a somewhat different per- spective on what I have already described in more traditionally psy- chodynamic terms; but my purpose will be to see whether this way of viewing our findings is fresher or more convincing.

To look at the artists of cluster 1 (the timid, informal, and expan- sive cluster) from this point of view, it would seem that they *attempt to weave a fabric of relationships that improve on the painful ones they had known much earlier.* Hands reach for a prize; good creatures subdue bad ones; an inviting landscape contains and protects; mankind is but the petals of a single flower; and a star hangs in the sky, admirable but alone. In some cases wish and doubt coexist, as in the highway home being a risky road as well. The interpersonal metaphor seems full of verbs such as moving, reaching, returning, uniting, dis- pensing justice, and containing; the interpersonal space seems to be one where reconnection with what had been lost takes place.

Cluster 2, constricted though equally informal, seems to reveal a world that ranges from the static to the threatening; it either stands still, though disconnected, or it risks being struck by a powerful force or rent asunder. The parents had been unreliable or clinging, and the present relationships are distant and tenuous; *it is as if the unreliabil- ity of the past and the disconnection in the present created a kind of map of the present that is equally unreliable and disconnected.*

Movement returns to cluster 3 (bold and flowing): dragons reach, rocks fall, vapors rise, forms blur or wiggle. The artists have parents who between them represent a kind of psychic completeness—one is emotional while the other is organized—and, more than in any other cluster, they are involved in an intimate relationship now; yet there, too, some of them experience both closeness and distance (five speak of being in a relationship with someone who is far away). *It is as if the form of their images represented both poles: the one parent provides the freedom of expression, while the other offers the encouragement*

*of coherence, and they are both close to and far from others, at some
distance that feels comfortable.*

Cluster 4 (bold, saccadic) is once again static: its images are dense
and piled up. We have seen that the image makers' life is one of cease-
less relating, of a compulsion to be with someone or to have sex, and
we have viewed the images' denseness as an aspect of the artists' drivenness. One can easily see how a life that needs to be filled in this
way translates into images that are themselves filled, but it seems a delicate paradox to note that *what may seem like movement forward in
life looks like stasis within the picture's frame; but then, repetition in
life is ultimately more like standing in place than moving forward, and
allowing yourself to be crowded is certain to make it difficult to move.*

The fifth cluster (timid, formal, and saccadic), is static as well, but
in a different manner and for different reasons. Elements are lined up,
centered, subdivided, labeled, or enclosed in a frame. The order seems
imposed, sometimes uneasily, from without. One can say that the artists
are perfectionists, as I have already, but one can also point out that
they were raised in intact families or families where a stepparent
replaced a biological parent successfully, and that the parents presented a united front to the child—and when one does so, *the pictures'
order becomes a symbol of the familial order; of an order that appears
to have been imposed from above rather than established through more
spontaneous ties.*

It is re-established relationships, not an established order, that we
find in cluster 6 (formal and flowing). *The forms are connected by
paths, by a consistent style, or by tension between similar but distant
elements.* Perhaps this is the cluster in which our sense of a map of the
interpersonal world finds its clearest illustration: the artists make clear
that *they wish to connect with nature and their family, integrate a feminine expressiveness with masculine control, or master the pain of a dis-
solved family.* To these artists goes the credit not only for the successful
images but for the clarity with which they described themselves.

The final cluster (abstract) is, in fact, no less clear an example,
although its map is different. The forms are produced by a hands-off
process and their appearance is abstract and mechanical; edges are either
sharp or deliberately blurred, or in one case merged by layering. In the
making we had sensed *a distance from the image and a reluctance to
touch it*, and in the artists we had noted an avoidance of emotional and
sexual closeness or an avoidance of relationships altogether; we also
noted the problematic boundaries with their parents. *Their interpersonal
map seems to have empty spaces and long distances between points,
unlike that of cluster 6, which was filled with roads under construction.*

THE SEVEN WAYS OF DOING ART AND
ARTISTS WE KNOW

The findings of a laboratory study become even more satisfying if it can be shown that they had been mirrors of the world outside. Each cluster should ideally correspond to the art and to the psychology of known artists; or, by way of illustration, of at least one artist. Even a quick perusal of the kinds of painters who would be represented in a history of art volume reveals a number of suitable names, and a check with their biographies reveals several lives that fit those of our participants—all except one, Marion Milner, who has done the biographical and self-critical work herself.

For the first cluster, which represented narrative informality in its form and compensatory longings in its motives, there should be little difficulty in finding suitable examples of narrative, since much art seen in museums has been narrative. It is informality that poses the greater challenge: if art has survived in museums, it is in part because it is memorable in its form. But if the informality one seeks in merely relative, then the paintings of **Henri Rousseau** (1844–1910) come to mind right away: lush jungle scenes with women nude or clothed, carnivals with their suggestion of romance, companionable animals sharing the jungle with humans. All of these appear as fulfillments of a relatively pleasant fantasy, as does Rousseau's self-portrait wearing the decoration of the *palmes académiques* which he never received (but another Henri Rousseau did), or the happy double portrait of his second wife and himself. Not quite all the fantasy is pleasant, of course; a bear may be attacked in the forest, or a tiger may lie dead at the feet of a hunter. But Rousseau's style, though admired in his day for its simple and straightforward organization of verticals and horizontals, is by art standards quite informal, just as his brushstroke is untutored and "primitive". Yet he was content with his work, and indeed admired it greatly (Vallier, 1962).

If his work looks like a clear example of wish fulfilling fantasy, his life is a little less clear in the matter of reparative wishes, but it is consistent with our first cluster in the matter of deprivation. The son of a tinsmith who—not a man of means to begin with—lost money and property to bad management, he had to move about a good bit with his family; their poor life contrasted ill with the memory of a heroic paternal grandfather and the presumption of a maternal connection to minor and distant nobility. His career as a minor tax official at the gates of Paris brought him no particular distinction, comfort or happiness, nor for quite some time did the painting career upon which he embarked at about 45 years of age. He was also known as a naïve and credulous man who was the natural butt of some of his friends' practical jokes. All in all, his life of penury, the loss of his first wife and seven of their eight children to an early death, and the shadow of ridicule that he could not have failed to perceive, afforded him few satisfactions— and it seems reasonable enough to assume that the exotic settings of some of his paintings and the glory and happiness of others gave him a glimpse of a happier and more interesting life.

The second cluster was summed up in the title, *Inhibited, disconnected forms and downcast, angry lives*. This style, too—with the caution that it may be difficult to find an artist who altogether subordinates form to subject matter—seems to find a parallel in the world of art. However partial the parallel may be, in this connection one can think of the life and work of **Alberto Giacometti** (1901–1966), known especially for his gaunt figure sculptures so evocative of anomie and loneliness. They are, of course, highly formal when contrasted with the figures produced by our second group. But the metallic limbs and torsos are knobby and rough, denying the body the graceful continuity we expect, and in this they are not unlike the disconnections we have seen here. His painted portrait of James Lord above all—discontinuous enough in its process, having been restarted on the same canvas at each of many sittings—elaborates the head and immediate background only, leaving the body a series of slashed, angry, disconnected lines (Lord, 1965).

The artist himself did have very tenuous relations with others, was mistrustful of emotion and deeply afraid of sexual intimacy, and although he idealized his mother, he was cruel, indeed sadistic toward other women in his life; he once carved his initials into his cousin's arm, and on more than one occasion screamed at and humiliated his wife in public (Wilson, 1985). Any complete account of his work would look at other matters as well, such as his foot fetishism and problems one might anticipate with his body image, but it is neither simplifying his life excessively nor denigrating his work in the slightest to point of out that a certain lack of inner cohesivenss and connection with others shows, in him as well, an affinity for discontinuous forms.

We turn to the *Bold, flowing process and the direct expression of emotion* that we saw as the nub of the third cluster. It seems closest to the robust, healthy style alluded to in Chapter 1, and in fact we would be hard put to find painting more intimately identified with vigorous graphic gestures than in the work of **Peter Paul Rubens** (1577–1640). The self-assurance, the swirling energy, and the sheer substance of his brushstrokes, as well as the twisting and diagonal movements of his personages, suggest just the kind of direct emotional expression that we have seen in this group. I have spoken of him as a model of the healthy artist, but here I wish to stress both the vigor of his style and his ability to feel emotion—the points of resemblance to our group. There is, of course, a profound difference: there is no hint of anger as a motivating force in Rubens, rather, a joy from life itself. But in other ways "boldness" and "flow" appear as much in his art as in his life. One is impressed by his closeness to his friends and his ability to be intimate, and one is equally moved by his capacity to mourn when bereaved. His inner life seemed as rich as his outer life was vigorous (White, 1980).

In the fourth cluster, whose images were dense and whose psychology revealed relentless control, the images were made of parts brought together into a dense pattern which reflected the artists' feeling of being driven; in some cases the need was for sex, in others love, but all shared the sense of being driven. Once again we may perform our little test in the world of art. Memory serves to propose **Max Beckmann** (1884–1950), the German painter often connected to the Expressionists, as one whose paintings are dense—dense in their composition, massive in their figures, heavy in their emotional charge—and coincidentally heavily dependent on black, just as some of ours had been. That is how they appear, and that is the effect they have on us; and we are curious whether the painter who painted them resembles our group in some significant way.

Fischer's critical study (1972) suggests that he does: like our subjects, he was driven. Brought up in a merchant family with no connection to art, he lost his father at the age of ten, but reacted to the loss by an obstinate determination rather than, for example, a wishful reparative fantasy or depression; and by the age of sixteen he knew that he was going to be an artist. As Fischer puts it while trying to explain Beckmann's meteoric success, "At the age of sixteen he was able, after a struggle, to enroll at the art school in Weimar. During the next year or two he behaved like a man bent on success at all costs. In 1903, after three years at Weimar, he considered his training completed, and in 1905 he proved, with an ambitious picture, that he was capable of getting on by his own efforts." We do not know if he was driven in other than ambitious ways, so we shall have to be content with a partial parallel. But if drivenness and relentlessness are crucial to this cluster's style, then Beckmann illustrates it rather well.

In the fifth cluster, the photographs with which the paintings started were modified by imposing an order upon them, and in eight of the eleven paintings flowers were present, suggesting prettification and a certain daintiness. I spoke of *Imposed order, inhibition, and the acceptance of parental standards.* Here I reverse the procedure and start with the psychology, because it has been so finely described in an auto-biographical study. **Marion Milner** (1900–1998) was a painter and psychologist who wrote a subtle and persuasive account of her discovery of her inner—genuine and emotional—artistic processes in the book *On Not Being Able to Paint* (1957). Feeling her own art to be blocked, and responding to a suggestion that she try drawings that rely more on free association than preconceived notions of what art should be, she discovered a world of aggressive, primitive, puzzling images which symbolized all that she had denied in her life and art, and all that might have made her work interesting and meaningful from the start.

It is her inhibited start that connects with our cluster. Her images had been realistic, peaceful, beautiful or pretty—the very stuff of what she thought art should be—and the psychology that underlay them was idealizing and repressive. The order and prettiness of her early images was imposed on an inner life of which she was unaware at first. In her own words: "So many of us are taught the way of offering the cave-man within us a model or exalted set of standards of how he ought to behave and then brow-beating or cajoling him into copying them as best he can. I had even thought that this was how one would produce pictures. I had intended something great and beautiful and studied the rules and then expected the results to follow from the excellence of the intention" (Milner, 1957, p. 91). That she changed as a result of her psychoanalytic work only underscores the close connection between her artistic form and her psychodynamics: her openness to affect, even highly unwelcome affect, allowed her to give up her idealizing and prettifying style.

The sixth cluster consisted of four artists who displayed a *Consistent style and the need to integrate.* It is not difficult at all to connect this cluster to the world of art. Until the twentieth century, art has always *been* art by virtue of its ability to integrate experience rather than merely portray it, and any reasonably well composed photographic image is adequate testimony to that. But to find the right parallel we need to look at artists in whose work integration is central; and here it is **Paul Cézanne** (1839–1906) that comes to mind.

The introductory chapter started with an epigram that spoke of Cézanne's artistic problem of establishing the points of contact between the elements of his late work, and the discussion that followed spoke of his problematic contact with others. In a recent work (1996) I have shown how deeply integrated Cézanne's landscapes were, and how attentively he searched for the evidence of the interconnections between their parts as he painted. His still lives were masterpieces of complex connections and resolved tensions. Yet this overriding concern and ultimate success was accompanied by a difficulty in sustaining relations with others. His relation to his wife Hortense was intimate only for a short while, and thereafter distant, carping and critical; his connection with boyhood friends, certainly intense until his maturity, was also eventually broken; and his relations with recent acquaintances were tenuous and easily interrupted by a touchy suspiciousness. Yet the word "contact" appears time and again in his late letters as the goal he wishes to achieve in his painting studies—and as the problem he finds hardest to solve.

Finally we arrive at the seventh cluster, where *abstraction* was connected with *avoidance and the search for firm boundaries*. Inadvertently, I had alluded to this dynamic in Chapter 1 when I spoke theoretically of a style in which both the life and the artist's work rely on rigidity of defense. We saw **Piet Mondrian** (1872–1944) as the embodiment of that style, and here I may offer him as a nearly perfect parallel to our cluster. Mondrian, the master of utterly unemotional abstraction, was as avoidant of fleshy reality in his art as he was abstemious in his life. The son of a Calvinist preacher, he was correct, neat, and fastidious in his habits, feared emotional and sexual intimacy and never achieved it in any form with anyone; and although quite capable of falling in love and idealizing, he was incapable of going beyond the initial enthusiasm and allowing himself to love. His preference for straight, angular movements in dance—he was an enthusiast of the dances of his time, which he preferred to the older, rounder, slower, and physically closer forms such as the waltz—was perfectly consistent with, and probably found its highest embodiment in, the late painting style in which straight lines and rectangles of primary color were thoughtfully and delicately balanced against each other on a field of white (Gay, 1976).

We may say, then, that in the world of art it is possible to find similar ways of making images, *connected to similar clusters of needs and ways of managing them.* I do not wish to overstate the matter: finding illustrative cases is satisfactory in its own right, but it does not tell us how many important styles of working it has explained and how many it has left out. Nor have the biographies gone into enough detail about the inner lives of the painters to cast any light on the "maps of the interpersonal world" that our participants allowed us to glimpse. We also can say very little about the role of sheer talent in affecting the relationship between the artist's life and his or her work; one would anticipate that it would complicate it, but whether it is by attenuating it or strengthening it no one can say at the moment. But, by such comparisons as these, the connection between the psychology and the style of the artist, which the biographical approach repeatedly suggests, is certainly strengthened.

My starting point had been the disparate patches in Cézanne's late work, and my question had been whether the difficulty he experienced in joining them at their "tenuous and delicate" points of contact was as much a personal question as an aesthetic one. Everything we have discovered here, from students who told us so much about themselves, suggests by analogy that it was. Artistic images can be made for many occasions and in response to many needs, but left alone to take what form they might, they will reveal the form of our inner world.

Appendix A

Psychological Analysis of the Clusters: A Partial Replication

Joseph Keiser and Kristoffer Berlin

By using cluster analysis, Machotka has ensured that his grouping of images is internally consistent—that within each cluster the images are formally similar and between clusters they are dissimilar. He has also argued that the personalities of the subjects are internally consistent and externally different, and on this basis concluded that the seven types of image clusters in fact stand for seven psychological approaches to image making. To have confidence in these conclusions, however, he wished to have an independent analysis conducted of a few of the clusters, and asked if we (Keiser and Berlin) would undertake it.

At the time they made the request, we were research assistants working with Machotka and Felton on a later research project which uses similar methods but asks different questions. Therefore, we knew their methods but had neither read the conclusions of this study nor heard of them indirectly. We were asked, we understand, because of our commitment to research and our familiarity with interpreting the personality protocols.

Our instructions were simple and phrased so as to keep our analysis as independent of Machotka's as possible. Due to time constraints, we were only able to work with four out of the total seven cluster groups, but we feel that our results are convincing even with this limitation. Our guidelines were to look at the images and interview protocols for each subject within these four clusters, code them on the psychological dimensions that stood out to us, judge the degree of internal consistency within each cluster, and offer our own interpretations regarding each cluster's specific features. In our analysis of successive clusters, we were also to verify whether, or to what degree, the clusters differed from the ones we had analyzed already. We were to work independently, and after compiling our notes on any given cluster, meet with Machotka and Felton to compare results.

Once we saw the consistency between our two analyses, we decided to write up the results together. Our results are presented in the order in which we analyzed the clusters, because the order of analysis certainly had an effect on the interpretations and perceptions of each successive cluster we looked at, i.e., while analyzing one cluster, we were actively comparing our results to previous clusters to find where they differed or were similar. Where needed, we have detailed our differences either in analysis or interpretation, and considered to what degree Machotka and we differed in perception, language, or interpretation.

Our results are very exciting in that they show that these clusters are indeed psychologically cohesive. They confirm that the cohesiveness results not from a human tendency to discern patterns where none may actually exist, because, if that were so, we would have found different patterns, which we did not. We wish to add that many of the subjects who had been briefed by Machotka and Felton about their profiles, agreed with the descriptions of themselves. This by itself does not reflect upon the consistency of the clusters, but it strengthens our belief that the profiles—which four of us have now developed—are valid portraits of the persons they intend to describe. Our conclusions regarding what we viewed to be the most important features of each cluster group will be presented with a description of how we worked and how we arrived at our converging analyses.

SEVENTH CLUSTER: ABSTRACTION, AVOIDANCE, AND THE SEARCH FOR FIRM BOUNDARIES

We turned first to cluster seven, whose images are characterized by abstract detachment. We (Keiser and Berlin) agreed upon two important psychological features of this cluster: that its members are both emotionally distant and have a difficulty expressing emotion. Both features can be seen in the subjects' lack of involvement with others and in the brevity of their intimate relationships. Many subjects reported having short (only a few months long) intimate relationships, or none at all. These features also mirror their parents' emotional distance from their children, and from one another (either distanced by divorce or a perceived lack of intimacy). Some examples of how several subjects describe their parents include "not talking to each other," "not much communication," and "they barely touch each other." We all placed somewhat different interpretations upon the import and origins of these features. Machotka observed the emotional distance expressed in the artwork itself in which abstraction functions as a means to avoid emotional material; as a defense against intimacy. This is different from Keiser's interpretation of cluster seven, which regards the abstraction not as a means to avoid emotional material but as an untrained and ineffective expression of emotions. Keiser in addition emphasizes emotional distance in the subjects' reported interactions with friends and family, and also with the interviewer—all of which may have been learned from their parents' distance from their children and from each other. Looking at the images, Berlin views the chaotic and unstructured expression of emotion as a reflection of emotional distance. Thus, we all agree that the subjects appear to dodge emotional material in order to avoid intimate contact with both the interviewer and everyday acquaintances.

We also agreed upon certain other features, but only as a result of discussion. For example, the lack of intimate involvement was given more prominence by Machotka, who noted that sex was not very important to these subjects and that for one it was just an obsessive ritual. Keiser and Berlin agreed with this in discussion, but had not noted it themselves. Although Machotka stressed the obsessiveness of only one subject, Keiser saw it to some degree in all of them, and Berlin emphasized a high amount of obsessiveness and a strong need for control over emotions—especially within social relationships.

Finally, we agreed with Machotka about the issue of personal boundaries. He found this issue in the blurred surfaces of the images and the "blurred" goals for the images themselves. In addition, he had noted it in the parents' inconsistency, absence of discipline and, above all, intrusiveness into the child's psychological space. We agreed with these observations of the subjects' childhood, though we gave it a somewhat different interpretation. For Keiser, the important matter was the lack of connection between the subjects and their families, and their struggle to find a way to regulate their connection to the world now. Berlin viewed these pronounced boundaries as a logical correlate of detachment. If these subjects had difficulty in both expressing and feeling their emotions, it would make sense to see distance in their intimate relationships, and boundaries between the subject and others. Berlin and Keiser agree that having no model of close relationships in childhood, these subjects now form and conduct their relationships by automatically establishing boundaries just as they learned to as children.

In summary, we all found cluster seven to be made up of participants who are emotionally distancing and inexpressive (in social settings especially). These subjects have issues concerning their connection with the world around them. In additon, we all agreed, though in somewhat different ways, that abstraction in their images was related to these psychological issues in their lives. Although the sixth cluster is also comprised of abstract images, these same dynamics were not found.

SIXTH CLUSTER: CONSISTENT STYLE AND THE NEED TO INTEGRATE

The first prominent feature that Keiser and Berlin found to be important in this group was that all of the subjects' parents were described as having ongoing, connected relationships. Some parents were divorced, some were still married, but all had maintained some sort of consistent relationship with each other and with their children. This is unlike cluster seven subjects who described their parents as distant and disconnected. Both Keiser and Berlin observed that the fathers in this cluster were very inexpressive of emotion while the mothers were caring and emotionally expressive. Many of their mothers were either primary caregivers or were simply emotionally closer to the subjects, while fathers were described as distant, unemotional, and even angry and abusive toward the subjects. Berlin regarded this contrast in parental roles as a very important dynamic, and Keiser postulated that this dual parental influence may have led these subjects to be verbally inexpressive of emotions, but able to effectively release their emotions using art as an outlet.

The sixth cluster is comprised of subjects who can control when and how they express themselves—and their expression is not chaotic (as is the seventh cluster) but is instead effective and healthy. The artwork in cluster six emphasizes composition and expresses a clearer intent than the chaotic and confused images in cluster seven. Although Machotka did not discuss these subjects as a group, their descriptions of the parents of each agree perfectly with these observations, as do their comments about the subjects' expressive uses of art.

In the process of discussing our separate analyses of cluster six we found that our agreement was not originally as clear as it had been with cluster seven. However, after discussing our separate views we found that we did in fact agree—but our terminology and focus had been different enough to blur our agreement. Berlin emphasized that although the fathers were either temperamental or controlling, in each case the parents provided at least one model to identify with as a source of strength. Keiser observed that connections within the family (between parents and between parents and children), although sometimes expressed through open and volatile arguing, seem to have been internalized by the subjects as a need to maintain a connection with the world (unlike cluster seven, in which creating boundaries was an emphasis). For this cluster art has become a method to safely build emotional connections with the world and to maintain other social relationships by such symbolic means of expression as well. Machotka emphasizes these subjects' attempts to integrate their emotional and interpersonal reality through a consistent style. This interpretation is consistent with Keiser and Berlin's description of a cluster in which the subjects' main issue is connectedness.

Comparison of Sixth and Seventh Clusters: Two Manners of Abstraction

While analyzing clusters six and seven we realized that two forms of abstraction were at work. In cluster six, the abstraction is more classically produced, meaning that the images are more formal and controlled. Cluster seven is comprised of images in which abstraction is relatively chaotic and untrained. There is little care for composition or clarity of expression in cluster seven. Although we each take a slightly different view of the reasons for abstraction to be present in these two clusters, we all agree upon what differentiates the abstraction between them. In cluster six the goal is to bring together a coherent image to better express what the subjects cannot otherwise say; this can be seen as reflecting this cluster's overall focus on connection. The images in cluster seven are disjointed because the subjects do not know how to connect, or how to express themselves effectively (whether through art or language). In both cases, emotional expression is an issue which comes forth as abstraction, but only in cluster six does the abstraction serve as an effective outlet.

FOURTH CLUSTER: DENSE PAINTING AND RELENTLESS CONTROL

When we met to discuss the fourth cluster we immediately became aware that we had come to the same conclusions, though from different angles of analysis. Keiser had focused more on the subjects' families and on the issues that family life might give rise to, while Berlin, Machotka and Felton focused more on the subjects' personalities. For Keiser, the emphasis was on the subjects' lack of control over the consistency of their relationship with their fathers. In other words, either the fathers would control when and how they might enter their children's lives, or their presence was regulated by uncontrollable factors. One father, for example, was indefinitely detained in Vietnam, while another worked, played golf, or watched TV, interacting with his child only when he was angry or drunk. The subjects' lack of control, often combined with some abusiveness, seems to have led to the development of a fear of life and a need to seek control over life's inconsistencies. Berlin observed that subjects subordinate everything in their lives to ambition as a means of maintaining control. This ambition may be a defensive style learned from having been raised in an emotionally and verbally abusive family. Berlin further noted that the form of control these subjects exerted on the world around them was obsessive in every case. If there was a difference in emphasis between us, it was that Keiser stressed the reasons for control and Berlin stressed its form. This is a dilemma to which Machotka alludes as well, but these observations are perfectly consistent in his emphasis on these subjects' relentless and obsessive defensive style.

Another factor we found to be important was these subjects' inability to express anger. Keiser did not directly see this element in the interviews, but he did deduce its presence from family histories contained therein. These families used anger as a means of punishment, manifesting itself within the family as rage. From this childhood experience, Keiser deduced that subjects would have learned to fear anger and bottle it up—until, just as with their parents, it would explode. Berlin found this inability to express anger directly within the interview transcripts. For example, many subjects described their fear of the repercussions of expressing anger, or were afraid of losing the control that they desperately need to maintain over their anger. Machotka did not emphasize an issue with anger, but it is implied both in his emphasis on being obsessive and in the discussion of some individual subjects.

All of the subjects in this cluster were rated by Berlin as having high levels of either motivation, ambition, diligence and/or work ethic. Berlin was quick to note that many subjects have done well academically and describe themselves as: "having high standards," "perfectionistic," "fearful of slacking off," "ambitious," "driven," "tenacious and diligent." Keiser views ambition as a means to compensate for the fear of having no control, while Machotka feels that each subject has a core issue that is threatening enough to require ambition as a defense. Each of our observations of cluster four include ambition as a key element.

FIRST CLUSTER: NARRATIVE INFORMALITY AND COMPENSATORY LONGINGS

Unlike the other three clusters we analyzed, this one consists of images that each tell a story, and quite without regard to any formal concerns. We all saw the subjects as motivated to find or create a "good" world, one that was better than that of their childhood. Unlike the subjects in other clusters, their concern is not in making sense of their past world but with creating a new and better one in which to live now. Berlin noted that the creation of a better world was not confined to the images they produced, but included being "good" people in their lives. For example, many subjects wish to become therapists or to serve a similar function in the world by helping others. Even the subjects from disciplines other than psychology, such as economics and creative writing, strongly shared this desire to serve their fellow human beings. Keiser, focusing on a developmental interpretation, observed that the subjects' only reference to their childhood personalities, for example, whether they were good or bad children, was completely dependent upon their parents' treatment of them; many of them seem not to have broken free of this social referencing yet. As a result, they hold on to, or have created, a dualistic, good/bad, view of the world, one which easily leads them to an involvement with religion (seen consistently only in this cluster), and to a view of the world in terms of black and white. In such a world they are, or try to be, the "good" people.

Berlin and Keiser's perspectives are more focused than, but perfectly consistent with, Machotka's emphasis on wish-fulfillment. Where Machotka notices a yearning in the images, unfulfilled wishes, or an idealized portrayal of the self, Berlin and Keiser witness a history which requires the subjects to try to live in a world which is better than the one they had known as children. Berlin interprets this as a need to find a balance between the restrictive childhood of their pasts and the possibilities of the present. Each of our analyses finds that these subjects wish to lead a relaxed life, free of restrictions, which is a reaction to the excessively strict and tense lives they had led as children.

Comparison of First and Fourth Clusters:
Childhood, Wish Fulfillment, and Drive

As with clusters six and seven, in which we detailed the function and types of abstraction at work, it seems relevant for us to compare and contrast the psychology of clusters one and four. In both, the subjects have endured some sort of restricted or abusive childhood that has impacted their lives as adults. In cluster four, the effect of this childhood experience takes the form of an intense drive to succeed. These subjects gain control and security in their lives by achieving goals and succeeding in their endeavors. It is almost as if these subjects were so disempowered during childhood that their adult lives are spent ensuring that they will never again be so vulnerable.

The subjects in cluster one, having had a similarly restrictive environment as children, feel as if they have a responsibility to ensure that others need not live as they had lived as children, by providing services that either empower or improve the lives of others. As cluster one wishes to empower others, the subjects in cluster four set out to empower themselves, but both act out of a need to control the world around them. These different manifestations of control seeking may be due to differing levels of severity in restriction and abuse during childhood.

In summary, we are satisfied that the clusters have an internal psychological coherence, and believe that other observers looking at these data would arrive at similar conclusions. We believe that we have not only described each cluster in a relatively objective manner, but that we have also come to sense which dynamics are the most salient in each and how they affect some of the differences—at times subtle—between clusters. Through the use of a somewhat unorthodox method of verification—both qualitative and unrestricted—we have both gathered support for Machotka's conclusions. In addition, we have discovered just how much can be learned from the study of images and interviews with the artists who create them.

Appendix B

Interview Forms and Statistical Tables

POST-IMAGE MAKING INTERVIEW

Participant ID:
Original image:
Title of transformed image:

1. Now that you have finished, would you care to comment on your picture?
2. Has it turned out the way you wanted it to?
3. How did you know when the image was finished?
4. Does it have a meaning?
5. Is it related to your life in any way?
6. Would you care to comment on the image-making process? What was it like for you?
7. Can you recall what first attracted you to this study?
8. Do you have any experience with computer graphics or images?
9. I would like to know a little more about your background in art:
   A. What has been your art making experience?
   B. Do you visit museums and galleries? (Is there something that stands out as the most influential? What was the most recent?)
   C. Are the any artists in your family? Who influenced your aesthetic development?

PSYCHODYNAMIC INTERVIEW

Instructions: These are topics to cover, not the questions themselves. You have had practice in asking them in a way that is comfortable for you. Make sure to probe and elaborate, and ask for specific examples.

Participant ID:

1. [Interviewer's impression of participant]
2. Age, size of family, birth order.
3. Marital status of parents.
4. Age of parents.
5. Father's occupation.
6. Mother's occupation.
7. Description of father (now and when you were a child).
8. In what ways do you resemble your father? In what ways are you different from him?
9. What is your relationship with your father like (now/then)?
10. Description of mother (now and when you were a child).
11. In what ways do you resemble your mother? In what ways are you different from her?
12. What is your relationship with your mother like (now/then)?
13. Whom do you identify with more, your mother or your father?
14. Parents' relationship with each other (now, and when you were a child).
14a. Expressiveness in family (e.g., love, anger).
15. Other important parental figures in your life (now/then).
16. Parental discipline (what kind? what did that mostly have to do with?).
17. Parental expectations (of behavior, goals, etc.).
18. What are your personal goals?
19. What role did religion play in your family?
20. How significant is religion to you now?
21. Are you in a (esp. intimate) relationship now?
22. What do you need in a relationship?
23. What are your relationships usually like? (E.g., long? short? committed? uncommitted?)
24. Do you have an idea of the ideal relationship?

25. Importance of love in relationships, in life. (E.g., how important is love for you in your relationships?)
26. Do you like romantic movies or novels? (Examples? Anything recent come to mind?)
27. Importance of sex in relationships and life.
28. How tolerant or intolerant are you? (Suggest a scale to start discussion).
29. How self-accepting or self-critical are you? (Suggest a scale to start discussion).
30. How do you deal with anger? (recent example)
31. Would you call yourself aggressive? (recent example)
32. Would you call yourself assertive? (recent example)
33. Do you like movies or novels with aggression or violence in them? (examples)
34. Would you say you are an emotionally expressive person? (In what way? Were your parents emotionally expressive?)
35. How spontaneous are you? (Impulsive? How do you react to surprises?)
36. What are your prominent fears?
37. If you had three wishes, what would they be?
38. Is there anything else, or anything to add to your previous answers?

Participant ID____   Rater____   Check if final rating_____   Date_____

IMAGE AND PROCESS ASSESSMENT

1 obliterates image __:__:__:__:__:__ preserves image
2 focus on process[1] __:__:__:__:__:__ focus on product[2]
3 small-scale working[3] __:__:__:__:__:__ large-scale working
4 mechanical __:__:__:__:__:__ hands-on
5 bold attempt[4] __:__:__:__:__:__ timid attempt
6 saccadic process[5] __:__:__:__:__:__ flowing process
7 dense effect[6] __:__:__:__:__:__ sparse effect[7]
8 bold effect __:__:__:__:__:__ tiid effect
9 stimulates emotional __:__:__:__:__:__ doesn't stimulate
response[8] response
10 downbeat mood __:__:__:__:__:__ upbeat mood
11 banal __:__:__:__:__:__ idiosyncratic
12 static __:__:__:__:__:__ moving
13 sharp __:__:__:__:__:__ diffuse
14 space accessible, deep[9] __:__:__:__:__:__ space inaccessible, flat

Purpose of image: 1 2 3 4 5

15 emphasis on form[10] __ __ __ __ __
16 concern w/ integrating own form[11] w/ original image __ __ __ __ __
17 emphasis on narrative __ __ __ __ __
18 concern w/ integrating narrative w/ original image __ __ __ __ __
19 emphasis on texture, repetition, pattern[12] __ __ __ __ __
20 emphasis on representation __ __ __ __ __
21 emphasis on realism __ __ __ __ __

[1] without apparent destination.
[2] working toward a destination.
[3] reserve "1" for work done only under magnification, 3 or less for any magnification at all.
[4] takes risks.
[5] straight, jagged, disconnected.
[6] judge from total surface area: many forms, messy, crowded, no visual resting points.
[7] judge from total surface area: empty.
[8] personal: "I am emotionally moved".
[9] is your vision moving into space? rate "1" only if unobstructed; if there are 2 planes, rate "4".
[10] formal relationships, focus.
[11] not elements.
[12] integrating textures, or achieving expression through textures.

Table 1. Loadings of Assessment Dimensions on Five Factors

	Image-based narrative	Timid	Flowing	Formal	Expansive
1 Preserves image	.48	.52	.09	.24	−.33
2 Focus on product	.49	.21	−.26	.00	.47
3 Large-scale working	−.27	−.08	.02	−.08	**.69***
4 Hands-on	**.54**	−.28	.41	.10	−.08
5 Timid attempt	−.06	**.88**	−.01	−.10	−.05
6 Flowing process	.28	−.34	**.72**	.11	.28
7 Sparse effect	.29	.22	.42	−.16	.25
8 Timid effect	.05	**.87**	−.05	−.21	−.01
9 Does not stimulate	−.22	**.80**	−.32	−.10	−.02
10 Upbeat mood	.08	−.15	.18	.20	**.56**
11 Idiosyncratic	.23	**−.78**	.31	.05	.11
12 Moving	.21	−.47	**.68**	.03	.15
13 Diffuse	−.23	−.05	**.72**	.13	−.12
14 Space flat	**−.67**	.15	−.29	−.27	.12
15 Emphasis on form	−.03	−.41	.00	**.68**	.24
16 Integrating form	.31	−.06	.25	**.73**	−.09
17 Emphasis on narrative	**.71**	−.44	−.01	−.36	.00
18 Integrating narrative	**.75**	−.20	.08	.06	.01
19 Emphasis on pattern	**−.62**	−.29	−.22	.39	.11
20 Emphasis on representation	**.85**	−.15	.04	.03	.04
21 Emphasis on realism	**.72**	.17	−.16	.35	−.02

Bold face: Defining variable.

Table 2. Mean Factor Scores of the Seven Clusters*

	Image-based narrative	Timid	Flowing	Formal	Expansive
Cluster 1 Expansive, informal, timid	0.70	**0.93**	0.30	**−1.12**	**1.39**
Cluster 2 Constricted, informal	0.01	0.47	0.24	**−0.74**	**−0.89**
Cluster 3 Bold, flowing	0.26	**−1.06**	**0.93**	0.07	0.00
Cluster 4 Saccadic, bold	−0.46	**−0.92**	**−1.35**	−0.02	−0.49
Cluster 5 Timid, formal, saccadic	0.58	**0.89**	**−0.81**	**0.87**	0.02
Cluster 6 Formal, flowing	0.06	0.13	**1.09**	**1.83**	0.10
Cluster 7 Abstract	**−1.08**	−0.03	−0.31	0.11	0.66

*Bold face: Defining variable. Negative numbers indicate opposite end of dimension: *abstract* vs. image-based, *bold* vs. timid, *saccadic* vs. flowing, *informal* vs. formal, *constricted* vs. expansive.

Table 3. Discriminant Analysis (First Cluster)

(a) Mean individual scores on each factor

Image title	Image-based narrative	Timid	Flowing	Formal	Expansive
Estate	1.16	1.77	−.65	−.52	.91
Highway Home	.98	1.11	.29	−1.52	.88
Saturn	.18	1.17	1.15	−.98	.89
Life	.86	.94	−1.10	−2.36	1.78
Yee World	.69	−.08	.01	−1.64	2.76
Sunset	.96	1.38	1.22	−.37	.53
Feeling	1.33	.06	.65	−.19	2.19
Flying Peachy	−.52	1.13	.88	−1.45	1.20

(b) Correlation (r) between individual scores and mean cluster scores

Image title	Clus 1	Clus 2	Clus 3	Clus 4	Clus 5	Clus 6	Clus 7
Estate	.95						
Highway Home	.99						
Saturn	.99						
Life	.99						
Yee World	.99						
Sunset	.99						
Feeling	.99						
Flying Peachy	.99						

Table 4. Discriminant Analysis (Second Cluster)

(a) Mean individual scores on each factor

Image title	Image-based narrative	Timid	Flowing	Formal	Expansive
Mosaic Flowers	−.98	1.17	−.08	−.17	−.54
Filtered Flowers	−.86	1.02	−.13	−.01	−1.27
Tapestry	−1.32	1.00	.66	−.95	−1.44
Mosaic Sky	−.10	1.69	.25	−.46	−.33
Society	.60	−.11	.23	−.77	−1.14
Goya	1.97	−.30	.33	−.91	−.98
Smudgie-pie	1.17	1.17	−.34	−1.00	−2.78
Lightning	−.55	.02	1.59	−.65	−1.23
Growing	1.77	−.42	−.16	−1.53	−1.86
Tears	.23	−.47	−.14	−1.42	−.57
Reflections	−.56	.98	.90	−.21	−.43
Monster	−.61	−.14	.54	−.91	−.76
Monogram	−.61	−.26	.05	−1.48	.05
Chanterelle	1.12	−.15	−.50	−1.02	−.01

(b) Correlation (r) between individual scores and mean cluster scores

Image title	Clus 1	Clus 2	Clus 3	Clus 4	Clus 5	Clus 6	Clus 7
Mosaic Flowers		.69					.19
Filtered Flowers		.84					
Tapestry		.99					
Mosaic Sky		.81					
Society		.96					
Goya		.93					
Smudgie-pie		.99					
Lightning		.59					
Growing		.99					
Tears		.96					
Reflections		.94					
Monster		.89					
Monogram		.87					
Chanterelle		.93					

Table 5. Discriminant Analysis (Third Cluster)

(a) Mean individual scores on each factor

Image title	Image-based narrative	Timid	Flowing	Formal	Expansive
End of World	2.33	−1.88	−.18	.73	−.46
Dragon Snow	1.66	−1.77	.05	−.41	.01
My Rooftop	.42	−2.12	1.50	−.06	−.76
Destitute Depot	.21	−1.28	1.58	.83	−1.12
Scribbles	.10	−.02	.86	.34	−.15
Garden of Eve	1.04	−2.14	.03	1.60	.56
Chocolate Swirls	−1.33	−.13	2.00	−.86	.63
Whirlwinds	.40	−.26	1.44	−.89	.40
Perceptions of	−1.21	−.92	.91	.03	−.47
Split	−1.68	−.85	.98	.24	.79
Scream	1.09	−.79	1.29	−.36	−1.49
Honeymoon	.26	−1.89	.79	.94	1.43

(b) Correlation (r) between individual scores and mean cluster scores

Image title	Clus 1	Clus 2	Clus 3	Clus 4	Clus 5	Clus 6	Clus 7
End of World			.99				
Dragon Snow			.99				
My Rooftop			.99				
Destitute Depot			.98				
Scribbles		.17	.70				
Garden of Eve			.89				
Chocolate Swirls			.92				
Whirlwinds		.17	.78				
Perceptions of			.93				
Split			.68				.30
Scream			.92				
Honeymoon			.97				

Table 6. Discriminant Analysis (Fourth Cluster)

(a) Mean individual scores on each factor

Image title	Image-based narrative	Timid	Flowing	Formal	Expansive
Banshees	−.52	−.93	−1.03	.56	−.08
War of Leaves	.98	−1.54	−1.53	−.82	−.06
Garden Tools	−.24	−1.24	−2.07	.18	−.20
Untitled Flowers	.10	−.02	.86	.34	−.15
Graffiti	−1.18	−.96	−.75	−1.32	−.94
Lost	.14	−.58	−1.77	1.27	−.69
Textural Abyss	−1.17	−.80	−1.26	−.50	−1.64
Psychedelic Village	−.99	−.93	−1.69	−.46	.56
Winterland	−.42	−.91	−.42	1.34	−1.09

(b) Correlation (r) between individual scores and mean cluster scores

Image title	Clus 1	Clus 2	Clus 3	Clus 4	Clus 5	Clus 6	Clus 7
Banshees				.89			
War of Leaves				.96			
Garden Tools				.99			
Untitled Flowers				.87			
Graffiti				.94			
Lost				.98			
Textural Abyss				.99			
Psychedelic Village				.87			
Winterland				.95			

Table 7. Discriminant Analysis (Fifth Cluster)

(a) Mean individual scores on each factor

Image title	Image-based narrative	Timid	Flowing	Formal	Expansive
Urbania	.95	−.40	−1.14	.70	.93
Suburbia	.89	.51	−.43	.67	−.19
Spectrum	−.17	1.16	−1.13	.86	.68
Persistence	.31	.54	−.29	.82	−.04
Waterfall	.50	−.96	−.75	−1.32	−.94
Wish you Were	1.85	1.27	−1.34	.47	.51
Garden of Eden	.78	1.00	−1.07	−.04	−1.06
Mine	−.24	.78	−1.02	.61	−1.15
Mieru	1.22	1.34	−.23	1.19	−.37
Framed Flowers	−.10	.89	−2.47	1.02	1.03
Mother's Garden	.40	1.81	.16	1.97	−.52

(b) Correlation (r) between individual scores and mean cluster scores

Image title	Clus 1	Clus 2	Clus 3	Clus 4	Clus 5	Clus 6	Clus 7
Urbania					.75		.21
Suburbia					.90		
Spectrum					.96		
Persistence					.91		
Waterfall					.87		
Wish you Were					.99		
Garden of Eden		.25			.74		
Mine					.71		
Mieru					.99		
Framed Flowers					.97		
Mother's Garden					.96		

Table 8. Discriminant Analysis (Sixth Cluster)

(a) Mean individual scores on each factor

Image title	Image-based narrative	Timid	Flowing	Formal	Expansive
Enchanted Sicily	2.29	.57	1.09	2.17	1.34
Colors	−.45	.16	1.66	1.47	.19
Fruit Tree	−.22	−.18	.94	1.93	−.49
Temple Cluster	−.69	−.44	1.76	1.79	.84

(b) Correlation (r) between individual scores and mean cluster scores

Image title	Clus 1	Clus 2	Clus 3	Clus 4	Clus 5	Clus 6	Clus 7
Enchanted Sicily						.99	
Colors						.88	
Fruit Tree						.92	
Temple Cluster						.89	

Table 9. Discriminant Analysis (Seventh Cluster)

(a) Mean individual scores on each factor

Image title	Image-based narrative	Timid	Flowing	Formal	Expansive
Fuzzy	−1.07	.45	.34	.43	−.15
No	−1.16	.47	.41	−.74	1.23
Choices	−1.32	−1.35	−.40	−.08	.85
Vein	−1.37	.49	.15	−.28	.10
Highpass	−.44	.10	−.89	.28	1.13
Axon	−1.10	−.02	−.86	.46	.13
Frustrated	−1.42	.09	−.79	−.67	.60
City of Dreams	−1.17	−.58	−.59	−.31	.99
Type on Flowers	−1.01	.26	−.11	1.48	1.51

(b) Correlation (r) between individual scores and mean cluster scores

Image title	Clus 1	Clus 2	Clus 3	Clus 4	Clus 5	Clus 6	Clus 7
Fuzzy							.73
No							.71
Choices				.24			.72
Vein		.22					.75
Highpass							.84
Axon							.71
Frustrated							.93
City of Dreams							.95
Type on Flowers							.85

References

Babbage, S. J. & Valentine, E. R. (1995). Musical responsiveness and blocked capacity for intimacy: A comparison of music and psychology students. *British Journal of Medical Psychology,* **68**, 269–277.

Clark, K. (1984). *The Nude: A study in ideal form.* Princeton, NJ: Princeton University Press.

Doran, P. M. (1978). *Conversations avec Cézanne.* Paris: Macula.

Dudek, S. & Marchand, P. (1983). Artistic style and personality in creative painters. *Journal of Personality Assessment,* **43**, 139–142.

Dudek, S. & Hall, W. B. (1979). Design philosophy and personal style in architecture. *Journal of altered states of consciousness.* **4**, 83–92.

Fischer, Friedhelm W. (1972). *Max Beckmann.* London: Phaedon.

Freud, S. (1907). Delusions and dreams in Jensen's "Gradiva". *Standard Edition,* **9**, 3–95.

Freud, S. (1908). Creative writers and daydreaming. *Standard Edition,* **9**, 142–153.

Freud, S. (1959). The Moses of Michelangelo. *Collected papers,* IV, 257–287. New York: Basic Books.

Freud, S. (1928). Dostoevsky and parricide. *Standard Edition,* **21**, 175–196.

Freud, S. (1959). Fragment of an analysis of a case of hysteria. *Collected papers,* III, 13–146. New York: Basic Books.

Gay, P. (1976). *Art and act.* New York: Harper.

Gedo, M. (1980). *Picasso: Art as autobiography.* Chicago: The University of Chicago Press.

Lanvin, M. A. (Ed.) (1967) (originally published in 1550). *Giorgio Vasari: Lives of the most eminent painters.* New York: The Heritage Press.

Lord, J. (c. 1965). *A Giacometti portrait.* New York: Museum of Modern Art (dist. by Doubleday).

Machotka, P. (1979). *The Nude: Perception and personality.* New York: Irvington.

Machotka, P. (1992). Psychobiography and visual creativity: four patterns. In Gerald C. Cupchik (Ed.), *Emerging visions: Contemporary approaches to the aesthetic process.* New York: Cambridge University Press.

Machotka, P. (1999). *Style and psyche: The art of Lundy Siegriest and Terry St. John.* Cresskill, NJ: Hampton Press.

McCrae, R. R. & Costa, P. T. (1997). Personality trait structure as a human universal. *American Psychologist,* **52**, 509–516.

Milner, M. (1957). *On not being able to paint.* New York: International Universities Press.

Murray, H. (1943). *Thematic Apperception Test Manual.* Cambridge, Mass.: Harvard University Press.

Segal, H. (1952). A psycho-analytical approach to aesthetics. *International Journal of Psychoanalysis*, **33**, 196–207.

Spitz, E. H. (1985a). *Art and psyche*. New Haven and London: Yale University Press.

Spitz, E. H. (1985b). A critique of pathography, Freud's original psychoanalytic approach to art. In Gedo, M. M. (Ed.), *Psychoanalytic perspectives on art*. Hillsdale, NJ: Lawrence Erlbaum (Vol. I, pp. 7–28).

Stokes, A. (1965). *The invitation in art*. London: Tavistock.

Vallier, D. (1962). *Henri Rousseau*. New York: Abrams.

White, C. (1980). *Peter Paul Rubens, Man and artist*. New Haven: Yale University Press.

Wilson, L. (1983). Review of James Lord, *Giacometti: A biography*. New York: Farrar, Strauss, Giroux. In Gedo, M. M. (Ed.), *Psychoanalytic perspectives on art*. Hillsdale, NJ: Lawrence Erlbaum, (1985) (Vol. III, pp. 309–314).

Wordsworth, W. (1950). Preface to the second edition of "Lyrical Ballads". In M. van Doren (Ed.), *Wordsworth: Selected poetry*. New York: The Modern Library.

Index